GOD SAVE

AMERICA

"American Standards of Behavior"

Sam Lybrand

Printed in the United States of America

ISBN-10: 0692549544

ISBN-13: 978-0692549544

10 9 8 7 6 5 4 3 2

Empire Publishing

www.empire-publishing.com

Table of Contents

GOD SAVE AMERICA

ABOUT THE AUTHOR

A wise man will hear, and will increase learning; and a man of understanding shall attain unto wise counsels. <u>Proverbs 1:5 KJV</u>

In my opinion America was created to be <u>run by ordinary people for ordinary people</u> so they could go about working hard and believing in Jesus Christ as their Lord and Savior. Thus a moral society was created for the American people to enjoy Life, Liberty and pursuit of happiness. Therefore a revolutionary country was established so that its citizens could be free to live moral lives without a government run church or a Pope telling everyone what to do and even what to believe. This book is written by an ordinary person of no significant notoriety that has been around the block a couple of times and has his own opinion of how our country should be run in order for our people to enjoy this beautiful country God has given us to call our own.

The Lybrand clan has been in America for some time and is not upstarts by no means. My first Grandfather came to Charleston, SC in 1753, from Germany, swore allegiance to the King of England and received a 250 acre land grant in upstate South Carolina, which is now Lexington County. He came with his wife, two sons and a daughter. This family multiplied and helped form four Christian Churches. From the clan came at least one Senator, two Mayors, a Superintendent of Education and a District Governor of the Lions Club. Four great uncles died in the Civil War and my direct ancestor had his arm blown off in the Battle of Atlanta and survived. Two streets I know of are name after two of these outstanding Lybrand's that served their community well. In other words my ancestors have been in the thick of America's growth since the beginning.

My name is Sam Lybrand and this book was written by me, as I see America from an older person's (78 years) point of view. Nowadays, many teenagers and young adults would dismiss my advice because they say I am from another generation. They seem to forget that it is my generation and the generations before me that are responsible for bringing this and other recent generation into being and paving the way for them to be doing and living the way they now live.

One thing that I keep thinking about is the thousands upon thousands of young men that died in the Pacific and in Germany to defeat pure evil. Many went into battle knowing that they might die and did it anyhow. What they did and who they defeated is the reason we have the free nation we have today. My soul cries out for all the lives lost defending our freedom and yet there are those among us that seem to be willing to give all this up for a little power and control over their fellow citizen.

The reason I did this research and wrote this book is because of the foolish and devastating decision some of my own kin and people in my own community have recently made that has caused them much hardship and heart aches. For ages mankind has had time tested instructions that clearly spelled out right from wrong. It would be a good bet that 95% of American households have these instructions in their home but they are never read or much less studied.

I am concerned that our people, especially our young people, have their nose stuck in one of these little electronic boxes and don't seem to notice what is going on around them. Thus they expect everything in life to be immediate or instant. They meet someone, kiss and then jump in the bed with them without thinking about the consequences of their actions. Many have no idea or knowledge of the past and how America got where it is today.

It is my objective to relate to you that an abundant and joyful life is available to all those who understand and live by the standards upon which this great nation was founded. To violate these principles will only lead to an unfulfilled life and a life lived in vain. There is abundant evidence that many in places of authority are currently violating time tested principles of what is right and what is wrong. America will speedily decline morally and strength wise unless our leadership grasps the error of their way and begun to lead better lives by make better life decisions.

I would be able to go to my grave smiling if only a few Americans that are living chaotic lives read this book and it made a difference in their life by the way they began to live after they had read this book.

Author's right to speak:
I came up on a hard working South Carolina Sea Island called Edisto Island. I had almost personal attention in small two room grammar school on Edisto. I was the only one in the seventh grade in grammar school. I graduated from a country high school with only 200 students in five grades. In high school I played the drums in the band, selected to go to Boy's State and in the 12th grade drove the school bus with an 82 mile round trip route and was paid $35.00 per month for doing so. I graduated from a prestigious military college and served as an officer in the U.S. Coast Guard, first in Puerto Rico and then in Miami, Florida. In Puerto Rico I stood 24 hour search and rescue watches, did port security, and explosive loading. In Miami I was a Marine investigator. In college I helped create a sailing team and was a member of the Bag Pipe Corp playing the Scott drum. Our band marched in the Eisenhower Inaugural Parade.

I am not politically active and I am the kind of citizens our Federal government is supposed to be representing. From my point of view our government is totally out of control and not representing our people in the way they should. Many in our government and courts seem to be pushing socialism which has proven over and over again that it does not work. We are messing with other nation's laws and practices that do not represent the American way of life where we use the Constitution to rule us. We also have forgotten that the Standards found in the Holy Christian Bible are where we get our guidance and stability.

My first job after I had served my draft obligations in the military was worked in industry for eight years in material control and purchasing. I also worked 41 years on straight commission in residential real estate. Between Coast Guard OCS and my first assignment I got married at the young age of 22 and over time we had three children that are all now successful in their own right. I am very active in Lions International and I am currently serving a fifth three year term as a Ruling Elder in the Presbyterian Church. The good Lord used me Initiated a large Bible teaching Presbyterian Church which began with 12 Elders and their families and grew to 1000 members in a short period of time. This proved many people's longing for the truth of God's Holy Words. I also had published around 500 newspaper articles in Southeastern newspapers called **American Standards of Behavior** dealing with how we should live according to God's commandment and precepts. These were published from 1995 to 2004 when I had to stop to fight pancreatic cancer which I survived.

As a point of interest, my first wife, who was a highly trained cancer nurse, who I married right out of college, died in 2000 with lupus and was sick for seven years which totally broke me financially and emotionally. We were living in Columbia, SC at the time. After I came to my senses, I went back home, which was Edisto Island, SC, and married a lady, in late 2000, whose husband has also died after a long illness. We went to grammar and high school together and dated some. Since I knew her and her family it seemed like the natural thing to do. We joined forces in a creek house she had inherited. Now between us we have seven children, three of mine and four of hers all in their late 40s and early 50s. Between them we have 15 grandchildren and one great grandchild. Therefore we now have a very active life keeping track of all these children and grandchildren. They make the past hardships seem a thing of the past. Life can have a happy ending when you wait on the Lord.

Another point of interest along the way in my life is that when my oldest son, became 18 he became uncontrollable and his behavior was awful and totally out of control. My wife and I put up with his cr*p for a year or so until I brought it to a head and put him on the street to fend for himself. He moved out and married a girl he met at a bar and moved in with her and her family. His father told him, "Boy you have to go to work!" Therefore, her dad did something I was unable to do. This son is now a successful banker and a lay preacher. He can mesmerize a congregation and brings in all kinds of business to the bank. Plus he is now my most attentive kid and keeps in close touch with us. I guess my point is that you cannot condone bad behavior or you will go down with it. I had no trouble out of the other two children because they saw what daddy would do. My youngest kid (now age 50) will shortly be ordained as a Deacon in a large Baptist Church in a town nearby. My daughter, the middle child, married a young man that is now high up in the government ranks, he contracts businesses and is now a ruling Elder in a Presbyterian church. I guess "Tough Love" is sometimes necessary.

Therefore I have had an active life and spent most of my life making a living using my own abilities and not depending on a regular pay check and yet making an above average living. Plus I have done my duty toward God and man with positions of authority. I am nothing special. I have just taken advantage of the opportunities that have presented themselves throughout my 78 years ordained for me to live so far. Now is time for me to pass down some of the knowledge I have gained so that others can profit from my experiences.

It is high time that the hard working American Christian stand up and tell the fanatics in our government and citizenship to begin to carry their own weight in helping to keep America strong and free or go to some socialist country where the government can tell them what to do and when to do it and leave us alone.

It is also high time our **American news media get off their high horse** and start being our "Watch Dog" or forth branch of government exposing the craziness now going on in America and get off this socialist kick. Our American news media, with a few exceptions, has lost it way and it is time they get busy helping to put America back on a more righteous track or just close up shop and die the natural death that is coming to them for not doing their duty toward the country that has served them so well over these many years.

As you can see I am just about ready to throw up when I think of what America could be and how it is being taken down the garden path by a few fanatics that we have tolerated far too long.

If you are an ordinary American Citizen, as I am, then please join with me in doing all you can with what clout you have in trying to keep America inhabited with hard working, moral people supporting themselves and their families with as little government interference as possible. Keep reminding everyone you see that America cannot stand alone without God's commandments and precepts.

INITIAL DISCLOSURE

In the past several generations the hard working moral ordinary American citizen had allowed members of the "Establishment" or "Reelection Cult" to almost bankrupt our country with excessive spending to assure their reelection.

In addition the past and current Administrations, members of our courts, members of Congress and our liberal news media have morally bankrupt the morals of the honest God fearing Americans. Therefore a 78 year old ordinary American citizen is speaking out the best he knows how, on what the solution to our national problems are in as simple of a way as he knows how.

Before you read one word in this book please be advised that it is not "Politically Correct". I have personally typed and compiled this book from the experience I have gained going around the block several times. I am the kind of American citizen our government is supposed to be representing and protecting in every way possible.

Therefore this book is written as you would expect a 78 year old to write who has no special training in English and how things should be written. The content is from my heart and a clear warning of things to come.

So read it slowly and try to get this message

and act accordingly as it was coming from advice from an older trusted successful grandfather. The future of America will be determined by how our American leaders, our news media and our citizens receive advice such as what I am presenting here. I have lived to see the decline in the moral values of our nation and the truth of it all hurts to the bone because of the loss of "how to live" **America is losing**. I cry for the future of my children and grandchildren. My wife and I have seven children, fifteen grandchildren and one great grandchild.

Therefore excuse the lack of style and format of a lively old man and profit from his years of experience living as an American (1937-2015) and has watched it decline, not in technology, but in moral decay.

Morals trump technology every day of the week! Morals will bring a country down much faster than the lack of technology.

This is not a goodie- goodie book it is just the plain truth!

DEDICATION

*For the wages of sin is death; but the gift of God is
eternal life through Jesus Christ our Lord.*
Romans 6:23 KJV

To all those men and women in the past that
have died fighting to continue the unique
freedom all Americans enjoy. Also to those who
are currently serving in the U.S. Armed forces in
all branches.

The next time you see the American Flag or
hear our National Anthem played, stop and thank
our maker for the brave souls that paid with their
life so that we may enjoy the gift of freedom. Also
remember all the young men that died in the
Second World War by the thousands that went
into battle knowing that they may die and they
did it anyway, to save our most valuable asset, our
freedom. We often forget what kind of life we
would be leading if Hitler and Japan had won the
Second World War. Therefore stop and think
who you are voting for in the next election as to
whether they have the interest of the American
people over their personal interest in just trying to
get reelected so they can stay on the government
dole or gravy train.

Then ask yourself what you have done,
individually, to help preserve this beloved

freedom that the entire world cries out to have. Do you belong to an active Civic Club that serves your community or do you belong to a church and help spread the good news of Jesus Christ and how America has prospered because of using His example to form our blessed nation?

The next time you see someone taking our freedom for granted, kick them in the shin as hard as you can to remind them what kind of nation we could be living under if it had not been for the forethought of our founding fathers to create such a unique and wonderful way to govern our people.

God bless those that have died so that I could be writing such a book without being put in prison for speaking my mind as I see, *__"How then shall I live?"__*

PROLOGUE

"It is written, 'Man shall not live by bread alone, but by every word that proceedeth out of the mouth of God.'"
Matthew 4:4 KJV

We all have inherited a beautiful nation conceived for the people and to be run by the people. We are a moral nation with hard working creative people free to do what is right and honorable in the eyes of God and man. But is there any evidence that our current population and leadership are extremely grateful to all those who died fighting for our unique freedom that the rest of the world are envious of?

Ponder on this and see how you (we) stack up.

FREEDOM

- As long as mankind has been in existence he has longed to be free.
- Freedom in America will become a distant memory without *Biblical Standards of Behavior* upon which our Republic was founded.
- Freedom comes at a price. Each generation must be willing to fight and some even shed blood to preserve our freedom.
- Isms such as socialism, progressives, and liberalism thinking must be purged by each generation for freedom to survive.
- Freedom is an individual responsibility. Each American is a link in the chair of freedom. One slack American could cause the chain of freedom to break.
- Do you even know what the Bible says about, *"How then shall I live?"* If not it is past time that everyone in America knows what God says about how we should live in order to keep freedom alive.
- Are you willing to pay all you have to preserve our freedom for the next generation? Many have!
- Your vote could be the vote that destroyed our freedom. Make it count! Know who you vote for!

Jesus said: *"And ye shall know the truth and the truth shall make you free."* **John 8:32 KJV**

Commentary:

The freest you will ever be is when you know what God expects of you and you likewise are abiding in God's commandments and precepts.

There is no law against being crime and sin free.

Pure foolishness!

The fool hath said in his heart, There is no God. **Psalm 14:1p KJV**

Many Americans that read this book or even think about reading it will consider it pure foolishness because it is about God and how He expects us to live. Many will say there is no God and no hell. They demonstrate this by the way they are living. There are approximately 2.18 billion Christians, or approximately one third of the world population, that at least believe there is a God so there must be something to it. From the attitude of many in today's America you would not think so.

We have four groups of people that are going to bring our nation down if they don't repent and begin to think of what they are doing to our blessed country. They are:

• Members of the Republican and Democratic parties that belong to the "Reelection Cult" now dominating Congress and only think about how they are going to stay in power. It is all about power. But they seem to have forgotten that, *"Power corrupts and absolute power corrupts absolutely,"* John Dalberg-Acton

• Academia. Many of our teachers and professors are running down America and are failing to teach our young people what made us great in the first place. Our parents are our first line of defense and many are also not teaching their children that they must become contributing citizens instead of relying on the government for everything.

• I hold the American News Media totally responsible for not doing their job as our fourth branch of government as our "Watch Dog" alerting our people when our leadership is about to take us down the garden path to destruction. For some strange reason the American News Media, with a few exceptions, are pro socialism and pro everything that is rotten and disgusting in America. If collectively they do not change and assume their responsibility they will be done away with. In a free society someone will realize the slackness of our American News Media and take up the duty of "Watch Dog." Mark my word this will happen and our news media, as it presently exist, will be no more. How sad!

• The last group are those who falsely believe that socialism is the way to government our people when socialism has failed every time it has tried. When you take the incentive to keep most of what you earn then production stops or is no longer operates as efficiently as it could be.

The following are statements made by Jesus Christ. Ponder on these verses as you read this book.

"And if thy hand offend thee, cut it off: it is better for thee to enter into life maimed, than having two hands to go into hell, into the fire that never shall be quenched: where their worm dieth not, and the fire is not quenched.

And if thy foot offend thee, cut it off: it is better for thee to enter halt (lame) into life, than having two feet to be cast into hell, into the fire that never shall be quenched: were their worm dieth not, and the fire is not quenched. **Mark 9:43-46 KJV**

CAN WE TALK?

*Happy is the man that findeth wisdom, and the man
that getteth understanding.*
Proverbs 3:13 KJV

When you go to a big city such as New York
City, the streets are full of people 24 hours a day.
When you ride on one of our busy interstate
highways you experience wall to wall cars going
who knows where. Then you ask, "Is there a God
in all this?" How many of these people going to
and fro even give any thought to the fact that
there is a God that expects them to be perfect in
every way? I wonder how many of all these people
aimlessly going here and there give any thought
that they were created in God's own image as a
living soul that will live for eternity either in
heaven or hell? Each of these thousands upon
thousands of people on the streets of New York
and on our busy highways are given a set of
standards to live by and those standards are found
in the Holy Bible. One of these standards is to
keep the Sabbath Holy and in recent years no
thought is given to this commandment. To most
it is just another day. Yet how many of our people
know what these standards are and the
consequences of not abiding in God's
commandments and precepts (rules of action or

27

conduct)?

We all are responsible for our conduct individually and as a nation. Each of those thousands upon thousands is individually responsible for how they live and what kind of witness they are. Like it or not we all are a witness whether we like it or not. Some are a good witness and others are a poor witness. Each person is individually responsible for their own actions. Another standard is to honor your father and mother. But how can you honor your father if he is never around as a large portion of our families now are absent of a father.

<u>Standards of Behavior</u> is how we are supposed to live our lives. These standards are explained throughout the Holy Bible. Even if you have never opened the Bible and learned what it teaches you are responsible for your actions because the knowledge of right and wrong are born in all of us as a living soul. One obvious example that we all know the difference between good and evil are that most crimes are committed at night or committed in secret hoping no one will find out. Very little crime or sin is committed in the open for everyone to see. Therefore in our heart we know that there is a God and that He hates sin. We may commit sin or crimes hoping no one will find out but God knows and unless we repent, receive Jesus Christ into our lives we are doomed because of our sins.

Then the question is asked, "How do we

know there is a God?" There is evidence that man originally came from Africa and then spread all over the Earth. But I have not seen any evidence that man came from a monkey or any other creature. How God created mankind will probably always be a mystery. The Biblical account of creation was man's best judgment of how it all happened and that is good enough for me. But it is clear that after it is all said and done God revealed Himself to Abraham the father of three great religions. These are Christians, Jews, and Muslims. They all go back to Abraham as their founding father. Common logic tells us that all these billions of people cannot all be wrong in believing there is a God. God also revealed himself to Moses and all the Old Testament prophets. He then came to Earth as Jesus Christ to show us how to live and to die for our sins. God has revealed Himself as God the Father, God the Son and God the Holy Spirit. God is a spirit and the creator. God created the Earth and all in the Universe and He created it out of nothing. The laws, elements and natural forces seen on Earth also apply to everything in the Universe and nothing just happens by chance.

Therefore knowing this our founding fathers created our Republic as a moral government to be run by moral people using the Holy Bible as their guide. If it was in the Bible it was already decided in their eyes. If it was not covered then they expected our elected representatives to deal with each problem in a moral and reasonable manner.

The tragedy of the current times is that every so often we get further and further away from God's standards without realizing that there are serious consequences for sinning against God since God created everything. He then created heaven and hell. Jesus tells us we don't want to spend eternity in hell in agony and torment.

God is a loving God and wishes none of us to perish but all to come to repentance. Therefore He came to earth to take the sin of the world upon himself and die so that everyone that believes in Jesus Christ would not die but inherit eternal life. But those who reject God's offer of salvation would be doomed to hell. I am not trying to judge anyone. I am just trying to tell the truth as I see it after years of studying the Bible and trying to live accordingly. But I repent a lot because I continually fall short and have to repent very often. Maybe by the time I get 100 I will have figured out how to live a perfect life.

How soon we forget the reality of things. Man cannot create or destroy anything. All he can do is change the form of things. Also man cannot create one living cell. He can cross breed living things but he cannot make a cat into a dog or cow into a whale. A cat has always been a cat and a dog has always been a dog no matter what anyone tells you. There a bunch of funny looking humans and dogs but there are all humans and dogs.

There is a spirit we call God. He cannot

tolerate evil because He is perfect in every way. Only He can create or destroy what He will. If lightening once struck some pond water millions of years ago and a living cell was created then what did it eat to survive and create its own kind? If you think about evolution you will have to admit it cannot stand the light of day. For things to evolve they had to start somewhere and for this to happen thousands of living cells had to have been created at one time so they could have something to eat and reproduce themselves. Wonder how long it took one cell to turn into an elephant? Foolishness!

Now think about the complexity of life here on Earth. Do you really think all this just happened? We have written proof that there is a God that created all this in Jesus Christ. He made a withered hand straight and created enough bread and fish out of a few loaves of bread and a couple of small fish to feed thousands. Christ told us that if we had seen or heard Him that we have seen God. Christ also told us that there is a heaven and hell and gave us a chance to choose which one we would spend eternity in. We are an eternal soul created by God in His likeness and our soul will live for eternity. This is a fact and we are currently living as though there was no God. The Bible calls this kind person's thinking fools.

I could go on for thousands of pages proving that there is a creator God. My point is that God hates evil and over the centuries nations have come and gone that have chosen to ignore God's commandments and precepts. We have had God's "Standards of Behavior" before us in the Holy Bible for centuries and yet we now choose to ignore them and go about our happy ways not giving any thought to our future without God's blessings.

Therefore if our nation does not repent and turn from their evil ways then we will be just another clouded memory of the past. Some other more deserving people will occupy our beautiful land. Our land will not go away but we can be replaced. Take the Middle East. How many different nations or peoples have occupied these lands over the history of mankind?

God is real and still runs His own creation and we'd better learn how He would have us live or be doomed. Christ came so that we could have life and have it more abundantly and yet we have rejected this great gift.

The Holy Bible is where we find the standards we are to live by. I hope we are smart enough to realize that before God just gets rid of us. A loving father disciplines his children and if the children continue to disobey him as they get older he has no option but to cut off the family support and put them on the street. This is called "Tough Love". A loving father cannot let one child disrupt the whole family. Many times during this will bring a child to its senses and again join the family as a contributing member. The Bible tells us that is just what God will do if we continue to disobey Him. He will just leave us to Satan so Satan can have his way with us. But God as our loving Father wish for none of us to perish by all to come to repentance.

Just think what kind of nation we would have if what I have just presented would be taught to all our people and they listened and tried to live a life pleasing to God. The Bible tells us that there is great joy in heaven every time a sinner comes to repentance.

What a glorious time it would be if all of America came to their senses and began to seek God's wisdom. **Have we lost all sense of reality?**

PROPHECY

Be not wise in thine own eyes: fear the Lord, and depart from evil.
Proverbs 3: 7 KJV

For sometimes now the following scripture has haunted me when looking at where America is headed in fear of its future for my children and grandchildren. I believe we are nearing a point of no return and have only a few years to determine whether we have a bright future or one that will lead to chaos and the loss of the freedom so many have died to preserve. Listen closely to these few scripture verses and see if they don't also apply to us. If you do nothing else with this book pass these scripture verses along to anyone that will listen, especially send them to our national leaders and ask them if they "give a dam" about what God thinks about the direction we are head without using His guidance.

Moreover all the chief of the priests, and the people, transgressed very much after all the abominations of the heathen; and polluted the house of the Lord which he had hallowed in Jerusalem.
*And the Lord God of their fathers sent to them by his messengers, rising up betimes, and

sending; because he had compassion on his people, and on his dwelling place.

But they mocked the messengers of God, and despised his words, and misused his prophets, until the wrath of the Lord arose against his people until there was no remedy.

Therefore he brought upon them the king of Chaldees, who slew their young men with the sword in the house of their sanctuary, and had no compassion upon young man or maiden, old man, or him that stooped for age: he gave them all into his hand. **2 Chronicles 36:14-17 KJV**

(* Another translation of this verse is: "*And the Lord, the God of their fathers, sent word to them again and again by His messengers, because He had compassion on His people and on His dwelling place.*")

It is my prophecy that if our American leaders and people don't turn back to the God of the Bible of whom our nation was founded then our future is bleak. This will be a direct result of our American leaders bowing to the desires of the heathens among us and bowing to their sinful desires in order to get reelected and thus staying in power to the point that their judgment has been clouded into believing we no longer need God's commandments and precepts as our **Standards of Behavior**. The above scripture that we have had for ages tells us what happens to sinful nations and I am retelling you again that if we don't turn from our sinful ways we will just be done away with and our land given to a more deserving people. Or God may even give our land to a pagan people to just get rid of us and for God to show us that He is still in command.

History clearly shows that God has gotten rid of sinful nations in the past. The overriding question before us is, "What makes us exempt from God's judgment?" The following scripture tells it like it is.

"The fool hath said in his heart, There is no God. They are corrupt, they have done abominable works, there is none that doeth good. **Psalm 14:1 KJV**

Our next national election will clearly show what our future will be. If we don't elect a righteous national leader that fears God then head of the mountains because our decline will rapidly began to decline and in a few years our freedom will be gone to never be regained again. God gave us a unique opportunity to rule ourselves and we blew it with one simple axiom. *"Power corrupts, absolute power corrupts absolutely."*

We need a President that will have enough spunk to have the Marine Band march around the Capitol once a week playing "Stars and Stripes Forever" to put some spirit and fight back into our government. Also have everyone in his Cabinet stand and sing "Onward, Christian Soldiers" before every Cabinet meeting to put

37

some spirit back in to America as to what kind of country we were designed to be. We don't want a Pope or State religion just the Word of God in our midst in everything we do and say. Listen closely to this old Camp Meeting song and see if it does not stir your soul to action.

Onward, Christian Soldiers

1. Onward Christian Soldiers, Marching as to war, with the cross of Jesus Going on before: Christ the royal Master Leads against the foe; forward into battle, See His banners go.

2. Like a might army Moves the Church of God; Brothers, we are treading where saints have trod: We are not divided, all one body we, One in hope and doctrine, One in charity.

3. Crown and thrones may perish, Kingdoms rise and wane, but the Church of Jesus Constant will remain; Gates of hell can never 'Gainst that Church prevail: We have Christ's own promise, And that cannot fail.

4. Onward, then, ye people, Join our happy throng, Blend with ours your voices in the triumph song: Glory, laud and honor Unto Christ the King; This through countless ages, Men and angels sing.

Refrain:

Onward, Christian soldiers, march as to war, with the cross of Jesus Going on before, Amen.

Our founding fathers built into our government checks and balances to avoid such and we blew these checks and balances with no term limits and not balanced budget amendment. I guess we all forgot that man was sinful and without God's commandments and precepts ever before us mankind would run himself into the ground and never know what hit him. Sinful man has shown his ugly head in America and unless we heed God's warnings we are doomed.

So what will it be? Continue on our sinful ways and die or pick up the Holy Christian Scriptures, which our nation was founded, and again begin to act like we are "Children of God."

I can see a glorious future for us but I can also see disaster lurking around the corner ready to pounce on us. If I had to weight the two I would lean toward disaster. Only righteous leadership can weight in above disaster. Can we muster righteousness? I sure hope and pray so!

INTRODUCTION

Treasures of wickedness profit nothing; but righteousness delivereth from death,
Proverbs 10:2 KJV

Before I get into the meat of this book I want it to be understood that the material I present to make my point, came from an extensive search of the internet and from my own experiences of living 78 years on God's green earth. Many will tell you that you cannot depend on what you find on the internet. Therefore do your own research on the things I have presented. I believe what I have presented at least makes my point and I again encourage anyone that reads this book to do their own search.

I am really concerned about the future of America and that we have left true Christian moral behavior behind in favor of anything goes. We seem to have forgotten that man is only truly free when he is living as close to God's commandments and precepts as possible and abiding by man's laws. It is my hope and prayer that many will read this book and begin to think of what they can individually do to help turn all Americans back to living according to how God would have us all live. Of course if you don't believe in God you'd better be right because agony and torment for eternity is a high price for being wrong. Think hard on this before you totally reject God and His influence on the lives of all of us individually and as a nation.

It is time someone came out and revealed or just comes right out and says it, **"We have too many fanatics trying to run our country."** It is not okay for our government to keep spending money we don't have and it is time we voted out all those who keep condoning the right to not work and stay home and let the government keep supporting them. It is past time for all American to begin to live according to strict moral standards and proud attitude toward hard work. If the fanatics want to be crazy let them move to a Communist Country and leave the hard working Christians run America like it was meant to be run, "One Nation under God."

It seems that every time I turn on the TV or listen to the radio I hear of another crazy bunch trying to justify some evil or running down someone that is trying to do right regardless if it is "Politically Correct" or not. Some things or lifestyles are just wrong, some are just plain filthy and not acceptable in a polite society. When people stop considering what is moral behavior and instead tries to justify what anyone wants to do even though it is immoral or filthy then the end is near. When did we begin to care about what some fringe group thinks is right and just went ahead and do what is right regardless of what the crazy group thinks or felt? Why should the minority start over-ruling the majority? The next time you see some fringe group causing problems just walk away and don't give them the time of day. They will stop being crazy when we begin to shun them. Shun someone long enough and they will stop their immoral or crazy thinking because no one wants to be left out of the mainstream of our society. If you want America to survive then pretend like the fringe groups don't exist and keep doing what is right in the sight of God and man.

An American biggie:

Like it or not we have the knowledge of God born in us. Note this scripture verse which confirms this.

Because that which may be known of God is manifest in them: for God hath shewed it unto them.
Romans 1:19 KJV

Instead of worrying about whose feelings we may hurt when someone that does not believe in God hears or sees scripture from the Holy Christian Bible, we should be worrying about their eternal soul. We sometimes forget that we were created a spiritual being in the likeness of God with an eternal soul that will live for eternity either in heaven or hell. Like it or not we all think about God. Also note the consequence of denying God.

But whosoever shall deny Me (Jesus Christ) before men, him will I also deny before My Father which is in heaven. **Matthew 10:33 KJV**

Can you think of a more devastating thing than being denied by God as an individual or as a nation?

Therefore think about who someone in the military calls upon when he is in a foxhole and an enemy is closing in on him and shooting at him trying to kill him? He surely does not call on some judge or politician that cannot see beyond their nose. He calls on God. It is said that "there are no atheists in foxholes." Also when a boat turns over at sea and its crew members are in the water alone, who do they call on and what promises do they make to God if He would only save them? They too are also surely not thinking about socialism and how it solves all of man's problems. They are thinking about God whose presence is born in them.

Then it stands to believe that any judge of political leader that tries to remove God's Holy Words from anywhere, public or private, must have lost their ever loving mind and is playing with our people's eternal soul by removing the possibility that they may never hear the Word of God and never turn from their wicked ways. Any judge or politician that tries to remove God's Holy Words from any sector of our society should be run out of America for violating the principles upon which America was established. If someone is offended by scripture they need to move to some none Christian country. Every time I see or hear about someone being jailed or ridiculed for talking or writing about God it hurts me to the bone because that judge or politician is going to suffer severe consequences. How about the rights of those that don't believe in God? The Bible clearly has an answer for them.

The fool hath said in his heart, There is no God. They are corrupt, they have done abominable works, there is none that doeth good, **Psalm 14:1 KJV**

The fool hath said in his heart, There is no God. Corrupt are they, and have done abominable iniquity, there is none that doeth good. **Psalm 53:1 KJV**

Note when a scripture is repeated several times it is obvious that God especially wants us to take note of this scripture.

With all this said, we are dooming many of our people's soul to hell by keeping the word of God from them. Again any judge or politician that is worried about hurting someone's feelings when they hear or see the Word or God should worry about their own soul for denying God in any way shape or form. I'll finish this biggie with these verses that put a high obligation on any leaders.

Let every soul be subject unto the higher powers. For there is not power but of God: the power that be are ordained of God.

Whosoever therefore resisteth the power, resisteth the ordinance of God: and they that resist shall receive to themselves damnation. **Romans 13:1-2 KJV**

If you are a judge or politician think hard on this and see where your soul is headed.

One of the real "Biggies" in America is those who call themselves Liberals or Progressive. It might seem great and right for the government to tell everyone what they can do and cannot do and to dole out the Federal treasury to every Tom, Dick and Harry that will not work or thinks he cannot work and the government should support them. These "Do Gooders" don't seem to understand that wealth only comes from producing a service or product. Someone either needs or wants the service or product and willing to pay for it. Keep in mind that the Government produces no wealth, if it were not for those who provide a needed service or a product, for a profit, that our people need then there would be nothing to tax and no money to run our government. Therefore it is would be nice to be able to support everyone with government money but where will the money come from to be so generous?

THE MOTIVE TO RECEIVE A PROFIT is what runs our economy. Why should a man invest his money in equipment to provide a service or product unless he sees that he can make a substantial return on his investment? Giving away the Federal treasury is surely not a very profitable idea. Where in the world did these fanatics get the idea that the government can give away the treasury when there would be no money in the treasury unless our people paid taxes into it?

Probably the most misunderstood concept is to distribute the wealth of the nation equally among all our people. When the incentive to keep the majority of what someone earns by providing a needed service or product is taken away from an individual or company then the individual will sit back and let the government take care of him. If it is a company and it cannot make a reasonable profit caused by the government then it will close down or start doing some illegal or underhanded way of doing business so they can keep the majority of what they make.

Therefore being a Liberal or so called Progressive is a flawed way of thinking. In fact these people are full of malarky if they think the government can leave the barn door open and survive!

Okay Liberals, if you want to be a liberal get yourself a nongovernment job on straight commission and give 90% of what you make to the government to dole out to those who will not work. If you don't like this then shut up and leave the producing of taxable wealth to the free enterprise system when one keeps what he makes by hard work and creative thinking.

Again when is the last time you heard one in our American News Media call one of our leaders "Righteous" in what they say and do. It seems that they have forgotten their role as our forth branch of our government as our "Watch Dog." With a few exceptions it seems that our news media sides with the liberals, socialist and fanatics. I guess being a good father, a community leader, a long time church officer and an outstanding civic club member is just not news worthy of printing or spoken about on the evening TV news. I guess looting, burning and riots that are out of control are the only news worth reporting. How about all the murders by blacks killing blacks? I guess that is not news. But let a white police even look hard at a black criminal and it becomes head line news. **How about it American News Media** do you believe in a future for America or are you only interested in what you can dig up about some person trying to do right in the sight of God and man? It is time the American News Media got back to doing what they are supposed to be doing, being our "Watch Dogs" and promoting hard work and moral living.

Are you living a contented and productive life? This book is about the standards we all should live by in order to live fulfilled, contented and productive lives.

Stop for a minute and let your mind wonder about where we came from and where we are going. Is this the direction we should be going? Then dreaming dreams and seeing visions of how things could be in America and in your own life. Then review with me what America has to offer.

First and foremost we are the freest people to

ever live on Earth thanks to the foresight of our founding fathers. We can travel from Florida to Maine, New York to California and no one will ever question why we are going to these places. We can even move from South Carolina to Texas and no one will question as to why you want to move. You can change from being a store clerk to running your own business and no one will question why you want to change jobs or careers. You can join a civic club or any church in America and no one will question why you want to join these organizations. You can get married or not get married. You can stay married or get a divorce and no one will question why you can do just about anything you want to do in America accept commit a crime or not pay your taxes. If you do either of these you will go to jail. You can even not pay your bills but you will end up on the street with no place to call home. Therefore in America you are free to do whatever is right. You will never be freer when you are trying to do what is right and honorable in the sight of God and man.

Here is another interesting thought. You are free to deny God and believe there is no Hell. Note this verse.

"He that believeth on Him (Jesus Christ) is not condemned: but he that believeth not is condemned already, because he hath not believed in the name of the only begotten Son of God." **John 3:18 KJV**

Do you think God is just kidding and you will not go to hell if you don't believe in Jesus Christ, by faith? If you think this you'd better be right. "Condemned" is a serious situation in any one's book. I am personally not going to take that chance and I have lived long enough to see the misery people that live their lives as if there were no God and no standards God asked us to live by.

On the bright side, go into a lighted room and try to put it out with darkness. It cannot be done. Darkness cannot overcome light. Therefore it is the darkness in our personal lives and the life of our country that bring chaos. Likewise, sin cannot overcome love. But love overcomes sin. A loving touch by someone that loves you will go a long way toward healing you when you are sick or just are having a bad day. **God is love** and we never should forget this and always be on the alert to share our love whenever the opportunity comes our way. A cool cup of water or a few dollars at the checkout line in a grocery store to someone that is short are acts of love in a small way but great to the one receiving the love at that point in time.

Where we seem to be going wrong is that we are worried about the feelings of a minority of our people that want to live different from what God expects of us and want us all to condone their crazy and sometimes unhealthy activities. What happened to the majority rules? In America we speak English. If you want to live in America then learn English. If you want to live in America we use the Constitution as our guide and we don't need or want some other form of government to run America. If you don't like our laws then go somewhere else and leave America to the Americans. If you don't want to work hard and just expect the government to take care of you then move to a socialist country where they will take most of your money but will provide for every need but you become a slave to that government. (But what happens when the government runs out of money, such as in Greece.) In America we believe everyone should work and provide for himself and his family and not depend on the government to provide for everything. Therefore it is my wish that the fanatics and socialist move somewhere else.

Oh, God has an answer to those that don't want to work. Note this verse.

"For even when we were with you, this we commanded you, that if any would not work, neither should he eat." **2 Thessalonians 3: 10 KJV**

Now let us think about what America has regarding her landscape. We have miles upon mile of beautiful beaches, great and majestic mountains, great sea ports and vast amount of farm land that can feed the nation and much of the world. We have many industries and businesses that provide jobs for many. We have many great cities where commerce can take place. We have a great military that protects us all and many citizens that are willing to serve in the military at the risk of their own lives.

America is made up of a diverse amount of people from every nation and language in the world that have come together as American to enjoy all that America has to offer its people. But when you move to America you must come in legally and leave the home land you left behind and become American and pledge your life and fortune to protection the freedom we all long to live under. Every one working together for the good of us all is what will make us great. If one person is hanging back and not carrying their load then the chain is broken and we are not as strong as we could be as a nation. The Love of God and abiding by His commandments and precepts is what will make all this happen.

We are supposed to have a government run by its citizens taking turns checking on our many government agencies to make sure they are operating efficiently and understand that they are **public servants** being paid to serve our people. Now it seems that our government agencies think we work for them and many have forgotten where their salary comes from. Their salary comes from the citizen's tax money they are supposed to be serving. When is the last time you heard the term "Public Servant" referred to when referring to a government worker?

With all this we must ask ourselves how we are going to keep all this going so we can enjoy this free American way of life for many generations to come. The answer is simple and yet we are dead set on making it complicated. The answer is that we all should live by a universal standard of behavior that has been available to mankind for centuries. These standards should begin to be taught in our homes and in all our schools, colleges and universities from the earliest grades to the most advance studies available in America. These standards should be ever present to all our citizens so there is no question on, **"How then shall we live?"** Any teacher or professor found running the American way of life down (a life based on moral behavior as found in the Holy Christian Bible) should be run out of the country. If they don't like and cherish America then they are living in the wrong country.

Ask yourself, "if America is so bad why do so many people from across the world want to come and live here?" I recently heard of a man that came here from a less free country and he was amazed at how we took for granted the freedoms we have and that everyone is not working hard to preserve this freedom. Another person I heard of that also came from another less free country stated that our success came from the fact that we have a church on every corner in every city and town in America and that most Americans do right without being told to do right. It is the people in America in leadership positions and even the average guy on the street that want to tear America down that this book is warning about. If properly brought up in Godly homes America is and can be the bright and loving light shining on the mountain top for all the world to see.

Over this past 4th of July celebration my wife and I had two of our grown children and their families, four adults and five children visit us. What a glorious time we all had together. We are very fortunate that both children are successful in their careers; they all go to church and take their children with them. They both have happy families, working together to make their homes welcoming and safe. What more can an old man want than seeing his children grow up, get married and become contributing citizens of our blessed country. I was raised this way, my parents were raised that way and as far back as I could find we are a moral working clan. This should be the wish for all our citizens. There is too much misery going on around us when contented and productive lives are possible for all our citizens. This is possible if we teach our children how God would have them behave and then live that way as an example to our children.

Again if America does not come to its senses, out vote the fanatics and put back into our society the standards this nation was founded upon we are in trouble and we soon will reach the point of no return. As Margret Thatcher, a past Great Britton Prime Minister said, "Socialism is great until you run out of everyone else's money."America needs to step back and really look at what got us to where we now are and make what adjustment are necessary to put us back on track to have America becoming a hard working moral nation. "In God We Trust".

WE HAVE REACHED OUR ZENITH

In Him (Jesus Christ) was life, and the life was the light of men. And the Light shineth in darkness; and the darkness comprehended it not.
John 1:3-5 KJV

Mankind has advanced technologically beyond our wildest imagination and great things are on the horizon. We have not even reached how far man can go. We have put a space craft on a comet and we have even sent a space craft to take pictures of Pluto billions of miles from us. We have advanced in medicine and means of transportation. Everyday new things come forth. Yet mankind has not advanced one single bit in our human relations. We still are trying to kill each other, one man is always trying to get ahead of the next man and many are not satisfied with their own wife and seek someone else's wife. We cannot even control our sexual desires. Without restrains mankind just self-destructs every time he tries to go it alone. With all his ability to create more and more advancement in technologically, medicine, etc., man is still an evil and sinful being. Thus for him to survive over a long period of time man must have leadership and restrains to know the limit of his activities. Without sound standards of behavior constantly brought to his attention man will self-destruct every time. History is full of countries and nations that are no longer with us because of man's sinfulness and lack of sound behavior.

As far back as you want to go, man has been ruled by a king or chief. Many other names have been given to these rulers that had absolute power over these tribes and countries. For eons of time man has longed to be free and safe in his own home and for his home to be his own castle. My ancestors came to America in 1753 to get away from princes that had absolute power over them. From one day to the next they did not know if they would be killed or their land or home was taken from them.

Then in 1776 our/my ancestors had finally had enough and they formed a government that was operated by the people, and for the people. They wanted to be as free as man can be. They formed a citizen controlled government where representatives were elected from the people to handle the business of the people. Checks and balances were put in place so that no one part of the government could have total control over the government or people. Our government was supposed to be a people led government.

As strange as it may seem, man in all his sinfulness is the most contented and happy when he is abiding by God and Man's laws. Man seems to get along best when he knows the rules he is to live by and then lives accordingly.

Now we have lost the reason we formed a people based government and have given too much power to a handful of people who are now members of Congress belonging to the "Reelection Cult". A large portion of those that were elected to represent our people now have lost the reason they were elected and now everything they do and vote for has to do with keeping them in power. These cult members also have no checks and balances and they just do what they please without regard to what it does to our people. In a sense we have gone back to the "King Rules a Kingdom" type government with a few deciding what goes on in America without any checks and balances. **We no longer have a government for the people.** This spells DOOM for America.

The age old saying, "When we fail to study history we are doomed to repeat it" is coming true in America. We have just about anything a person could desire. We have electronics coming out of our ear in every form imaginable. We have just about every time saving device we could ever want. Our standard of living is some of the highest in the world and people from all over the world want to come to America. You name it and America has it in some form or the other. Yet we have forgotten that man is sinful and as far as we know, has been since recorded history began. Without restraints this sinfulness of man has caused him to eventually fall by the wayside in disgrace.

I am afraid America has reached the zenith of civilization in our behavior and now we have beginning to die from being too, "Civilized". We seem to have lost sight of what makes a country strong and great. Many have become so spoiled that they feel entitled to sit around and look for the frailty in everyone else except themselves. We Americans as a whole have become cold and without love when it comes to our unborn. Making abortion seem it is a simple medical procedure rather than a human life created by God. Some groups worry about some spider or small fish and give no thought to the fact that a baby in the womb is a miracle from God. We have forgotten that we were created in the image of God and that our soul is eternal and will live forever either in heaven or in hell. Yes, hell. We keep trying to create life or understand how life started on Earth when the Bible already has explained all of this to us. We have forgotten that there are dire consequences to sin and nations have fallen when they totally ignored God's commandments and precepts. Sin is not on our radar and our destruction will come when everyone is drinking and making merry. But if we are ignorant of the existence of God and we cater to people that have no fear of God; our morals and integrity will eventually cause us to fail as a society. In our laziness we want everything now and want to be gratified now. Working hard and saving for what you want is out the door in today's generation. "Now" is the mindset of everyone today. We get in our cars and push a button and the car starts and off we go. We are in a generation of fast food, high speed internet and microwave ovens. Even in modern day relationships, this mind set carries over. Our young people kiss and jump in the bed to see if they like each other with no thought of what will happen to any children that comes from these encounters. We are a society of instant gratification. Plant a garden and wait for the harvest seems crazy in some people's minds. Thank goodness we still have farmers in America or we would all starve.

On the other hand we Americans are reelecting the same old tired representatives that want to stay in power indefinitely and do so by promising about half of our people they would kept on the government dole forever. No thought is given to where the money comes from to keep all these people dependent on the government.

We are supposed to have two political parties, the Democratic and Republican parties with two different points of view on how our government should operate but they both are the same because they don't want anything to change. Spend, spend, spend without any thought of the future and where the money will come to support all these programs are given no thought or consideration because it might upset their attachment to the government, and their easy life.

My wife and I have a house cat that just showed up at our house one day about eight years ago and said, crying, "Would you feed me?" Of course we did and we then obtained a cat that just came from who knows where. At first to show her gratitude for taking her in she started cleaning up our yard by killing all the rats and mice. She was a holy terror when it came to the rats in our yard. As time went by she came into our house and began sleeping on the easy chair and when it came meal time she was first in line. She stopped catching rats and showing her gratitude for us feeding her. The next thing we knew she began to sleep with us and I made the mistake of giving her canned cat food that I bought for her instead of giving her table scraps. Now she wants only a special kind of cat food and now sleeps 90% of the time. She only wakes up to be feed. She is now fat and can hardly get around. What does this sound like? She is perfectly capable of feeding herself with all the rats and mice around our house but since she had found the gravy train she has taken full advantage of it. I keep my house cat around because every now and then she sits in my lap and purrs like I am the only person in the world. She votes for me and I love it.

What do you think would happen to our household if we had 100 house cats to feed? We would soon be broke and could not even feed ourselves. Now think about our government. We have millions of people we are feeding and they are not contributing to our nation's wellbeing. How long do you think our government can keep up this outpouring of funds to people that are not contributing to our nation regardless of the reason.

America has now found itself with many elected officials that are acting like me when it comes to my house cat. They have made house cats out of many of our people by not requiring one thing from them in turn for feeding them with a lifestyle the rest of the world would love to have.

Have we reached our zenith? I would say we have already gone over the top of civilization and are on the other side. I offer the rest of this book as to the solution to our survival into the next ten to twenty years and beyond. All of America have to start pulling together for the good of us all (all working and no one on the government dole) and taking a serious roll in seeing to our future. All this bickering and who's on top has got to stop and every man, women and child have got to start pulling their own weight. I am sorry if some feel they have been mistreated or left behind. Tomorrow is another day you can begin to make a place for yourself using the opportunities now available to all of us. If you are interested look at many other countries and you will find that the opportunities which are in America are better than most places in the world. It is up to us as individuals to get involved and start cleaning up our behavior, waste and fraud that is now going on in America so we all can say we are proud to be Americans.

GOD OF OUR FATHER'S, WHOSE ALMIGHTY HAND

And when they (Jesus and His disciples) had sung a hymn, they went into the Mount of Olives
Mark 14:26 KJV

After the Last Supper, Jesus and the disciples sang a song. Over the centuries church congregations have been also singing hymns as part of their worship service. They are an inspirational part of the service. Some more spirit lead congregations really put their heart and soul into singing the old hymns. I love to hear the spiritual congregations sing. They really stir my soul and leave me with a warm feeling like I have been in the presents of God. Therefore I am including a hymn that meant something to me after each chapter. Even if you don't go to church and need a little uplifting then get yourself an old hymn book and begin reading some of these time tested hymn. I believe you will find it time well spent. Also hymns back up what our standards of behavior should be.

Here is the first of the hymns I am offering as a spirit lifter in this book. The music for this old hymn is especially moving. It would be worth your time to try to hear it played and sung by a choir the first chance you get.

God of our Fathers, Whose Almighty Hand...

1. God of our fathers, whose almighty hand Lead forth in beauty all the starry band of shining words in splendor through the skies, Our grateful songs before Thy throne arise.

2. Thy love divine hath led us in the past; in this free land by Thee our lot is cast; Be Thou our ruler, Guardian, Guide, and Stay; Thy word our law, Thy paths our chosen way.

3. From war's a alarms, from deadly pestilence, Be Thy strong arm our ever sure defense; Thy true religion in our hearts increase, Thy bounteous goodness nourish us in peace.

4. Refresh Thy people on their toilsome way, lead us from night to never ending day; Fill all our lives with love and grace divine. And glory, laud and praise be ever Thine. Amen.

THE COST OF FREEDOM

The merciful man doeth good to his own soul: but he that is cruel troubleth his own flesh.
Proverbs 11:17 KJV

I would venture to say that if you asked most Americans why we are so free when many people living in other countries are not as free they would not have a good explanation. If we are to keep our beloved freedom we need to start educating our children and even our citizens about the millions that have died to protecting our freedom. The actual numbers of those who died in our many wars need to be taught to our children over and over so that they would not take for granted that their freedom may not always be there if they don't keep their ear to the ground as to what is going on. It is often said that we can lose our freedom in one generation if our parents and schools do not keep telling our children what it takes to maintain our freedom.

I am often reminded that I lost four great uncles during the Civil War and my great, great, great Grandfather lost his arm in the battle for Atlanta during the Civil War. In his company 53 men died, 23 by disease. This was a horrible war and if the North had not won we would probably have less freedom now that we had before the war because we would have had two small weak countries instead of one large powerful country to protect our freedom.

During the Second World War many young men went to battle over needed Pacific Islands to bomb Japan with knowing they may die because so many had died before them. They did it to protect and to preserve our freedom. These numbers of diseased young Americans need to be taught to our students so they would not take their freedom for granted. During the Second World War there were very few American families that did not experience the loss of one or more of their love ones. One of my first cousins was in one of those long Japanese marches in the Pacific and survived but he had to be taken care of the rest of his life because it just about fried his brain because of the mistreatment. Ask his mother and father what our freedom cost them.

Now we must fight the radical Muslims that want to take over the world and are killing thousands of people and vow to come after us. If we don't fight them and destroy them our freedom will again be out the door.

Therefore each generation must fight and spill blood to protect and preserve our freedom. If we don't keep teaching each generation about the cost of freedom we will lose it because they will not know when a threat comes and will not be prepared to give their very lives to protect their families and the communities they depend on for their support and survival.

Freedom is not free, pass it on!

And when they (Jesus and his disciples) had sung a hymn, they went into the Mount of Olives. **Mark 14:26 KJV**

When Morning Gilds the Skies

1. When morning gilds the skies, My heart awaking cries, May Jesus Christ be praised! A like at work and prayer To Jesus I repair, May Jesus Christ be praised!

2. Does sadness fill my mind? A Solace here I find, May Jesus Christ be praised! Or fades my earthly bliss? My comfort still is this, May Jesus Christ be praised!

3. The night becomes as day When from the heart we say, May Jesus Christ be praised! The power of darkness fear When this sweet chant they hear, May Jesus Christ be praised!

4. Ye nations of mankind In this your oneness find. May Jesus Christ be praised! Let all the earth around Ring joyous with the sound, May Jesus Christ be praised!

EVIDENCE OF OUR HERITAGE

A fool despiseth his father's instructions: but he that regardeth reproof is prudent.
Proverbs 15:5 KJV

There is much evidence in Washington, DC of what our founding fathers wanted us to use as our **"Standards of Behavior."** Therefore I am including some of the sayings they left behind in as what they had to say about things. Also there are many inscriptions, carved in stone, in and on our many Federal buildings left behind for us all to see and remember.

If what we find is true then why have we now disregarded our heritage? Has our national leadership and our American News Media lost their ever loving minds and now let Satan rule?

Seriously look at what I have presented and then ask yourself, "Why have our America leadership decided to disregard what God has to say about, 'How then shall we live?'" If you had to cross a river and there were two boats to choose from to cross over, one sound and another rotten and leaking, which one would you choose? It seems that we are now disregarding the sound doctrine found in the Holy Christian Bible, upon

71

which our nation was founded, and have chosen the leaky craziness of the minority of citizens that want to live unhealthy sinful lives and want us to condone their ways that will lead to their eternal damnation. We must ask why with all the evidence left behind by our founding fathers.

These are only a few examples, do your own research and make your own decision on how our founding fathers wanted us to live as a country.

The U.S. Supreme Court Building:
Many would have you believe that the U.S. Supreme Court Building has no religious sayings or figures. You be the judge. Here are few points of interest.

• John Jay, who was the very first Supreme Court Justice said,

"America should select and prefer Christian as their rulers."

"Providence has given to our people the choice of their rulers, and it is their duty – as well as privilege and interest – of our Christian nation to select and prefer Christians for their rulers."

"The Bible is the best of all books, for it is the word of God and teaches us the way to be happy in this world and in the next. Continue to read it and to regulate

your life by its precepts."

• From Justice Joseph Story during a Harvard speech in 1829 we find the following.

I verily believe Christianity necessary to the support of civil society. One of the beautiful boast of our municipal jurisprudence is that Christianity is a part of the Common Law. There never has been a period in which the Common Law did not recognize Christianity as laying its foundation."

• From U.S. Supreme Court decision in Church of the Holy Trinity v United States – 1892 - we find this ruling.

"Our laws and our institutions must necessarily be based upon the old and embody that teaching of the Redeemer of mankind. It is impossible that it should be otherwise, and in this sense and to its extent our civilization and our institution are emphatically Christian. ... This is a Christian nation."

• Statue of Moses, who is considered our first law giver, is on the Supreme Court building.

• There are two large doors inside the Supreme Court building with the Roman numeral from one to ten representing the Ten

Commandments.

• Thomas Jefferson worried that the courts would overstep their authority and instead of interpreting of law would begin making law – An oligarchy, the rule of few over many.

The Washington Monument:

Embedded into the cap of the Washington Monument are the words **"Laus Deo"** which means "Praise be to God."
As you climb the steps to the top there are plaques with messages you find along the way. Plus other features that will give you the thinking of those at the time it was built.

• On the 12th landing is a prayer offered by the city of Baltimore; on the 20th is a memorial presented by some Chinese Christians; on the 24th a presentation made by Sunday School children from New York and Philadelphia quoting Proverbs 10:7, Luke 18:16 and Proverbs 22:6
Note: The city of Baltimore's prayer reads like this:
"May Heaven to this union continue its beneficence; may brotherly affection with union be perpetual; may the free constitution which is the work of our ancestors be sacredly maintained and it administration be stamped with wisdom and with

virtue."

Here is what the proverbs say that were presented by New York and Philadelphia:

Proverbs 10:7 KJV_He is in the way of life that keepeth instructions: but he that refuseth reproof erreth.

Proverbs 22:6 KJV_Train up a child in the way he should go: and when he is old, he will not depart from it.

Luke 18:16 KJV_But Jesus called them unto him, and said, Suffer little children to come unto me, and forbid them not: for such is the kingdom of God

Numerous other Bible verses and religious acknowledgements are carved on the blocks of the wall. Here are a few.

"Holiness to the Lord."

"Search the Scriptures."

"The memory of the just is blessed."

"May heaven to this Union continue its beneficence,"

"In God We Trust."

• When the cornerstone of the Washington Monument was laid on July 4th, 1848 deposited within it were many items including the Holy Bible presented by the Bible Society.

Capitol Building:
• "In God We Trust" is prominently displayed in both the United States House and Senate Chamber.

• Around the top of the walls in the House Chambers appears images of 23 great lawgivers from across the centuries, but Moses (The lawgiver, who according to the Bible- originally received the law of God.) is the only lawgiver honored with a full face view, looking down on the proceedings of the House.

• In the Rotunda is artwork showing Christopher Columbus prayer service; the Baptism of Pocahontas and the prayer and Bible Study of the Pilgrims.

• In the Cox Corridor of the Capitol are the words, ""America, God shed His grace on thee."

• At the east Senate entrance are the words, "Annuit Coeptis." (Latin for "God has favored our undertaking.") Also over the south entrance, "In God We Trust."

Jefferson Memorial
Here are a few of the quote in the Jefferson Memorial:

"We hold these truths to be self-evident: that

all men are created equal, that they are endowed by their Creator with certain inalienable right, among these are life, liberty, and the pursuit of happiness." -From the Declaration of Independence.

"*Almighty God hath created the mind free, All attempts to influence it by temporal punishment or burdens ... are a departure from the plan of the holy author of our religion ... No man shall be compelled to frequent or support any religious worship or ministry or shall otherwise suffer on account of his religious opinion or belief, but all men shall be free to profess and by argument to maintain, their opinions in matters of religion. I know but one code of morality for man whether acting singly or collectively.*"

"*God who gave us life gave us liberty. Can the liberties of a nation be secure when we have removed a conviction that these liberties are the gift of God? Indeed I tremble for my country when I reflect that God is just, that his justice cannot sleep forever. Commerce between master and slave is despotism. Nothing is more certainly written in the book of fate than that these people are to be free, establish a law for educating the common people. This it is the business of the state and on it general plan.*"

Lincoln Memorial

The Gettysburg Address

"Four scare and seven years ago our fathers bought forth, upon this continent a nation, conceived in liberty, and dedicated to the proposition that 'all men are created equal".

Now we are engaged in a great civil war, testing whether that nation or any nation so conceived and so dedicated, and long endure. We are met on a great battle field of that war; we come to dedicate a portion of it, as a final resting place for those who died here that the nation might live. This we may, in all propriety do.

But, in a large sense we do not dedicate – We cannot consecrate – we cannot hallow, this ground – the brave men, living and dead, who struggled here, have hollowed it, for above our poor power to add or detract. The world will little note, nor long remember what we say here, while it can never forget what they did here.

It is rather for us, the living, we have be dedicated to the great task remaining before us – that from thee honored dead we take increased devotion to that cause for which they have gave the last full measure of devotion – that we have highly resolve these dead shall have died in vain; that the nation, shall have a new birth of freedom, and that government of the people, by the people, for the people, shall not perish from the earth

Commentary:

I especially included Lincoln's famous speech because we need a **"new birth of Freedom"** from so much government involvement in our lives and for the statements "of the people", "by the people" and "for the people" because we now have professional politicians running things that are more interest in getting reelected and seeing just what they can get out of being on the government dole instead of seeing after the business of the nation. It is our people's fault for keep voting in these members of the **<u>"Reelection Cult."</u>**Only by requiring more of our people and educating them of how our Republic should be run and what standards we should operate by will any change happen in America.

Something to think about:

• Fifty-two of the fifty-five founders of the Constitution were members of the established Orthodox Church in the colonies. We also owe a debt of gratitude to all of those who signed the Declaration of Independence because most suffered greatly for signing this document that eventually secured our freedom.

• Congress printed a Bible for America and said, "The United States in Congress assembled...

recommend this edition of the Bible to the inhabitants of the United States ... A neat edition of the Holy Scriptures for the use of schools."
United States Congress 1782

• Congress passed this resolution: "The Congress of the united States recommends and approves the Holy bible for the use in all schools."
United States Congress 1782

There was much, "To Do" about the availability of Bibles during this period. A Mr. Robert Atiken petitioned Congress for permission to print English Bibles. Therefore he got permission and printed 10,000 Bibles. I understand that 30 or so of these Bible are still around. Here is another resolution I found given by Congress on this matter. I suggest you do your own study and research on this matter because it seemed very important to our founding fathers during this time. Here is what I found.

"Whereupon, RESOLVED, that the United States in Congress assembled highly approve the pious and laudable undertaking of Mr. Aitken, as subservient to the interest, as well as an instance of the progress of art in this country, and being satisfied from the above report of his care and accuracy in this executive of the work, they recommend this edition of the Bible to the inhabitants of the United States, and herby authorize him to publish this recommendation in the manner he shall think proper."

• By law the United States Congress adds to U.S Coinage, *"In God We Trust."***United States Congress 1864**

• **This statement was in the original Harvard University Student Handbook in 1636:**

"Let every student be plainly instructed and earnestly pressed to consider well the main end of his life and studies is, 'to know God and Jesus Christ, which is eternal life' (John 17:3), and therefore to lay Christ in the bottom, as the only foundation of all sound knowledge and learning. And seeing the Lord only giveth wisdom, let everyone seriously set himself by prayer in secret to seek it of Him, (Proverbs 2:3)

• Let me end this section with this all important Proverb.

"The fear of the Lord is the beginning of knowledge, but fools despise wisdom and instruction. **Proverb 1:7 <u>KJV</u>**

Commentary:

It is obvious from all the engraving on Capitol building and all the references to the Bible listed above (a short list) that the Bible was important to our founding fathers as was the Decoration of Independence and even the Constitution as our **"Standards of Behavior."** It also comes out that our founding fathers did not want a church state or the government telling anyone that they had to believe anything or worship any particular way. They also did not want a Pope telling them what to do and how to run their country. But I am convinced that if anyone really studies the thinking of our founding fathers it would be obvious that they wanted us all to live as close as we possibly could to the commandments and precepts found in the Bible as our **"Standards of Behavior."** This thinking seemed to have served our country well for many generations.

I grew up in the 40s and 50s and the Bible was still in the forefront of all of us during that time. In the military college I graduated from we were marched to chapel every Sunday morning and the band played once a month to put importance on going to hear God's words on a regular basis. We went by the code of "Duty – Honor – God and Country." If you violated any of these principles or knew anyone that violated these principles and did not turn them in you were immediately kicked out of college. Now it is "Duty – Honor and Respect." And you don't have to go to chapel. I guess the college leaders don't see a need for God's Holy words any longer. Plus I guess they don't need a strong and moral country backing them up. Their excuse is that the government now makes it illegal to call on the name of God in any government supported institutions. I guess those that are trying to kick God out of everything will spend eternity in agony and torment in hell unless they repent and mend their evil ways.

Now the question before us all is, "Why do we now consider anything quoted from the Bible as being on the same level with curse words? **Do we no long fear God and have we forgotten there is a hell?**

We have a bright future ahead of us but we will certainly not get there leaving God out of everything in fear that God's Holy words may hurt some uninformed person's feeling and not worry about their eternal soul. Instead of removing the mention of God everywhere we need to make sure that every American citizens know everything that is in the Holy Christian Bible so they will not have an excuse that they did not know what "Standards of Behavior" that have been our guide since the creation of these United States of America.

"For the word of God is quick, and powerful, and sharper than any two-edged sword, piercing even to the dividing asunder of soul and spirit, and of the joints and marrow, and is a discerner of the thoughts and intent of the heart. **Hebrews 4:12 KJV**

And when they (Jesus and His disciples) had sung a hymn, they went into the Mount of Olives
Mark 14:26 KJV

For the Beauty of the Earth

1. For the beauty of the earth, for the glory of the skies, For the love which from our birth Over and around us lies; Lord of all, to Thee we raise This our hymn of grateful praise

2. For the wonder of each hour of the day and of the night, hill and vale and tree and flower, Sun and moon and stars of light: Lord of all, to thee we raise this our hymn of grateful praise.

3. For the joy of human love, Brother, sister, parent, child ; Friend on earth and friends above, for all gentle thoughts and mild; Lord of all, to thee we raise this our hymn of grateful praise.

4. For Thy Church that evermore Lifteth holy hands above, Offering up on every shore Her pure sacrifice of love; Lord of all, to thee we raise this our hymn of grateful praise.

5. For Thy self, best gift divine, To our race so freely given; for that great, great love of Thine, Peace on earth and joy in heaven; Lord of all, to Thee we raise This our hymn of grateful praise. Amen.

AMERICA'S STANDARD OF BEHAVIOR

Train up a child in the way he should go: and when he is old he will not depart from it.
Proverbs 22:6 KJV

Again from the onset of this book many will say I am crazy to believe what I believe and what I am about to present. But if one has an open mind they will agree with me and begin to see where America is headed (to the trash heap if we don't change quickly.)

To begin with I looked up on Google what our founding fathers used as their guide in forming our blessed nation called the United States of America. Guess what? They used the Holy Christian Bible. Yes, the Christian Bible! Of course there's more of what I have presented but these quotes get my point across. Read and reread these quotes and let them sink in and then take a look at today's society and weep for America. But on the bright side, America has a great future if we will only get back to the basic standards revealed in these quotes.

Here are some of what our past President's thought about the standards found in the Holy Bible? (These quotes came from a Google search of the internet. There are two of these quotes I put in red because I think they are significant and should be taken note of. Look for them and ponder their importance to us today.)

"It is the duty of all American to acknowledge the providence of Almighty God, to obey His will, to be grateful for His benefits, and humbly to implore His protection and favor." - **George Washington – 1789 ~ 1797**

"Of all the dispositions and habits which lead to political prosperity, religion and morality are indispensable." - **George Washington**

"True religion affords to government it surest support." - **George Washington**

"It is impossible to rightly govern the world without God and the Bible." - **George Washington**

*"We do well to wish to learn ~ above all, the religion of Jesus Christ **in our schools**."* - **George Washington**

"We beseech [God] to pardon our national and other transgressions." - **George Washington – Thanksgiving Proclamation 1789**

"Oh, eternal and everlasting God, direct my thought, words and work. Wash away my sins in the

immaculate blood of the Lamb and purge my heart by thy Holy Spirit. Daily, frame me more and more in the likeness of Thy Son, Jesus Christ, that living in Thy fear, and dying in Thy favor, I may in thy appointed time obtain the resurrection of the justified unto eternal life. Bless, O Lord, the whole race of mankind and let the world be filled with the knowledge of Thee and Thy Son, Jesus Christ." - **George Washington ~ Prayer**

"The Declaration of Independence laid the cornerstone of human government upon the first precept of Christianity." - **John Adams -1797-1801**

"The general principles on which the fathers achieved independence were the general principles of Christianity. I will avow that I then believe and now believe that those general principles of Christianity are an eternal and immutable as the existence and attributes of God." - **John Adams**

"Our Constitution was made only for a moral and religious people. It is wholly inadequate to the government of any other." - **John Adams**

"I have examined all religions, and the result is that the Bible is the best book in the world." - **John Adams**

"God who gave us life gave us liberty. Can the liberties of a nation be secure when we have removed a conviction that these liberties are the gift of God? Indeed I tremble for my country when I reflect that God is just,

that His justice cannot sleep forever." - **Thomas Jefferson – Jefferson Memorial -1801-1809**

"The Christian religion is the best religion that has ever been given to man." - **Thomas Jefferson – Jefferson Memorial**

"The first and almost the only book deserving of universal attention is the Bible. I speak as a man of the world and I say to you, "Search the scriptures." - **John Quincy Adams, Sixth President**

"[The Bible} is the rock on which our Republic rests." - Andrew Jackson -1829-1837

"In regards to this great Book (the Bible), I have but to say it is the best gift God has given to man. All the good the Savior gave to the world was communicated through this book. But for it we could not know right from wrong. All things most desirable for man's welfare, here and hereafter, are found portrayed in it." - **Abraham Lincoln- 1861-1865**

"We the people are the rightful master of both Congress and the courts, not to overthrow the Constitution but to overthrow the men who pervert the Constitution." - **Abraham Lincoln**

"Whereas, the Senate of the United States, devoutly recognizing the Supreme Authority, and just Government of Almighty God, in all the affairs of men and of nations, has, by a resolution, requested the President to designate and set apart a day of national prayer and humiliation." - **Abraham Lincoln**

"If you take out of your statue, your constitution, your family life all that is taken from the Sacred Book, what would there be left to build society together? " - **Benjamin Harrison, 23rd President**

"The foundation of our society and our government rest so much on the teaching of the Bible that is would be difficult to support them if faith in these teachings would cease to be practically universal in our country." - **Calvin Coolidge-1923-1927**

"The strength of our country is the strength of its religion convictions. The foundation of our society and our government rest so much on the teaching of the Bible that it would be difficult to support then if faith in these teaching would cease to be practically universal in our country." - **Calvin Coolidge**

"I believe that the next half century will determine if we will advance the cause of Christian civilization or revert to the horror of brutal paganism." - **Theodore Roosevelt- 1901-1909**

"The Bible is the one supreme source of revelation of the meaning of life, the nature of God, and spiritual nature and needs of men. It is the only guide of life which really leads the spirit in the way of peace and salvation. America was born a Christian nation.

America was born exemplify that devotion to the element of righteousness which are derived the revelation of Holy Scripture." - **Woodrow Wilson – 28th President**

"We cannot read the history of our rise and development as a nation without reckoning with the place the Bible has occupied in shaping the advance of the Republic. Where we have been the truest and most consistent in obeying its precepts, we have attained the greatest measure of contentment and prosperity." - **Franklin D. Roosevelt-1933-1945**

"The fundamental basis of this Nation's law was given to Moses on the Mount. The fundamental basis of our Bill of Rights comes from the teaching which we got from Exodus and St. Matthew, from Isaiah and St. Paul." - **Harry S. Truman-1945-1953**

"This is a Christian Nation," - Harry S. Truman

"The National was established by man who believed in God ... You will see the evidence of this deep religious faith on every hand." - **Harry S. Truman**

"Without God there could be no America form of government, nor an American way of life. Recognition of the Supreme Being is the first, the, most basic, expression of Americanism. Thus, the founding fathers of America saw it, and thus with God's help, it will continue to be." - **Dwight D. Eisenhower-1953-1961**

"Of the many influences that have shaped the United States into a distinctive nation and people, none may be said to be more fundamental and enduring than the Bible." - **Ronald Reagan-1981-1989**

"Of the many influences that have shaped the United States into a distinctive nation and people, none may be said to be fundamental and enduring than the Bible." - **Ronald Reagan**

"For centuries the Bible's emphasis on compassion and love for our neighbor has inspired institutional and governmental expressions of benevolent outreach such as private charity, the establishment of schools and hospitals, and the abolition of slavery." - **Ronald Reagan**

"The Congress of the United States. In recognition of the unique contribution of the Bible in shaping the history and character of this Nation, and so many of the citizens, has by Senate Joint Resolution 165 authorized and requested the President to designate the year 1983 as the Year of the Bible." - **Ronald Reagan**

"Inside the Bible's pages lie the answer to all the problems that mankind has ever known. I hope America will read and study the Bible." - **Ronald Reagan**

In reading all these quotes by so many

Presidents one must ask, "Why did many of our past presidents think so much of the Bible and why did they use it as a model to form our Republic?" Do you think they knew something that we are ignoring today and thus we are reaping the whirlwind without knowing why? My research tells me that something changed in America around the beginning of the 1960s. The question is why? Could it be that we started listening to the wrong influences? Maybe we started listening to the bleeding heart big mouths with more ignorance than wisdom when we should have shunned them and not have given them any recognition other than they were fools in their behavior. Being called fools and not getting any notoriety will stop a lot of foolishness!

Let me first tell you what I think our founding fathers found worth coping in the Holy Christian Bible. Before I give you my opinion let me quote some scripture that has meant a lot to me over my short 78 years here on planet Earth. It has been my observation that you can never learn all that God is trying to tell us in the Holy Christian Bible. I have been going to church all my life and the older I get the more I see why God wants us to know all these things, Plus I see the results of many who are living unfulfilled lives because they are living contrary to how God would have them live their lives. I have been impressed by several Bible study groups of older men that I have heard about that have spent five or more years just studying Romans. As I get older my prayers are answered in Scripture plus the Holy Spirit is ever present in my life and He constantly is telling me what to do and what not to do because I have many evil thought that seem to come out of nowhere. One minute I am thinking about things of God and the next minute my mind takes me off in the wrong direction. Then the Holy Spirit brings me back, If you are honest with yourself you will realize that there is a warfare going on in your mind for control of your soul. But if you are well learned in the Holy Scripture the Holy Spirit always wins. If you are not regularly studying the Bible you might want to give it a try.

For copyright reasons I am using the King James Version of the Holy Christian Bible, abbreviated as **KJV** as I have already done at the beginning of this book is because it is not copyrighted. If you find some of the King James translation Scripture passages hard to understand then refer to a more modern translation. But if you really analyze each verse in the King James Version of the Bible as compared to a modern version you will find they say the same thing. Over the centuries, God's Holy word has never changed. You cannot justify sin no matter how you cut it and what God considers sin is clearly defined in the Holy Christian Bible. As I will state several times I am 78 years old and I am typing and doing my own research and recording what I have learned and experienced over the past many years of my attending Bible studies and pondering how God would have me live. I have actually had what I considered a vocal answer to several of my prayers that have come to pass in real time yet I still sin. Because we all sin we must take it to God. And be reconciled with a circumcised heart. What I have that many would long to have is contentment because I know without a doubt where I am going after my death. When you hear someone tell you they are saved, then you must wonder what they are saved from. They are saved from God's wrath because He cannot tolerate sin and those that do not accept God's offer of salvation through their acceptance of the saving grace of Jesus Christ by faith, they will have to answer for rejecting their saving Grace. Of course all sin can be forgiven if you repent and ask for forgiveness. Again if you deny God your sins will not be forgiven. If you are a thinking person I cannot see why you would want to reject God's offer of salvation.

In many people's book I should be mad at the world. Let me give you a few highlights. Not long into my first job out of the service my boss got laid off along with the whole department. I was rehired in another job to train their people and required to stay in that position while others got promoted above me. In my next two jobs the product in the plants I was working became obsolete and the plants closed. I then went into real estate so I could control my own destiny. In real estate I immediately became very successful and purchased a large house on a golf course with six bedrooms. At age 51 the Good Lord got my attention and humbled me with a very serious open heart surgery. When I came home from the hospital I could not lie down without blacking out. I was put back in the hospital in ICU with fluid around the heart. I stayed in ICU for four days to get the fluid off my heart. Not long after I recovered from the heart by-pass Blue Cross Insurance Company cancelled my health insurance and said I had used all my insurance. A little later my wife of 34 years came down with Lupus and was sick for seven years, three of which was in a nursing home that resulted in totally breaking me. During this ordeal I came down with a serious ulcer and put in the hospital from the stress of sick wife and bills piling up. The final blow came when I was supposed to have four real estate deals to close netting me $15,000.00 and they all fell through in one month leaving me totally broke. During this time I ended up selling my dream house and all our furniture trying to pay bills and staying afloat. I ended up with no money, no house, no furniture because I had to sell it to pay for medical and nursing home bills. In a relative short time I went from a high flying Realtor to totally broke. I ended up living with my son and sleeping on his couch with the dog. I guess I was lucky to have a son that would take me in.

During the ordeal with my wife I was going to a real estate appointment and was stressed to the hill. I asked God for a project to get my mind off my troubles. I know that God was somehow sitting in the car with me, and He said, "Would you agree that if you did not have a working knowledge of the Bible you do not have the knowledge to live a contented and productive life?" I immediately answered and said, "You'd have to be crazy to not agree with that." He said, "See what you can do about that." This still haunts me and it is partly the reason I am writing this book. As a result of this challenge I wrote and had published around 500 newspaper articles published in local southeastern newspapers called, **"American Standards of Behavior"**_dealing with how God would have us live. These papers printed my articles on the inside of their front cover. I did this weekly for 9 years. Be careful what you ask God for He might give it to you. At least the project gave me something to seriously think about during my wife's long illness.

Along the way during my real estate time the good Lord used me to help start what is now one of the largest Bible teaching churches in the area I sold real estate. In a short time we went from 12 Elders and their families (I was one of the Elders.) to 1000 members, there was a real need for the Word of God to be preached.

After my wife passed away I was able to get

back on my feet and I later remarried. Not long into our marriage I came down with pancreatic cancer and was told I had only a five percent chance of living and would probably die shortly. This was in 2004. I had an operation to remove the cancer and took six months of chemo. Here it is 2015 and I am still alive. Meanwhile, President Obama came to office, and with the "changes" he and his mess managed to shut down my market and I had to quit selling real estate because it was costing to sell real estate. Now my wife and I live on what little Social Security brings in. But we have a large garden and we eat a lot out of the salt water creek our home is located on. We now spend most of our time in church work in an old country church that has been active on our island for the past 325 years. I am currently serving my second three year term as a Ruling Elder in this old church. After going totally broke and stripped of my pride I am contented in my situation which many would consider meager in today's standards.

Without a sound knowledge of the Bible and a strong will to live I would have just given up. But I am now content in my situation and we use what we have and do not long to be anything otherwise. Do you think many of our founding fathers also knew the feeling of the love of God and that we can survive anything with Christ on our side?

I have included this to show that life is not all peaches and cream but that you can get through it all by knowing you will end up spending eternity with Jesus Christ if you hold fast and don't give up until you draw your final breath. Now let me get back to trying to explain where our standards of behavior come from.

Here are a few scriptures to try to give you some idea of why our founding fathers used the Holy Christian Bible as their guide for establishing our glorious Republic. These are some of my favorite verses that have meant a great deal to me over my many years of studying the Bible.

In the beginning God created the heavens and the earth. **Genesis 1:1 KJV**

The fool hath said in his heart, there is no God. They are corrupt. They have done abominable works, there is none that doeth good. **Psalm 14:1 KJV**

Blessed is the man that walketh not in the counsel of the ungodly, not sandeth in the way of sinner, nor sitteth in the seat of the scornful.
But his delight is in the law of the Lord; and in his law doth he meditate day and night.
And he shall be like a tree planted by the river of water, that bringeth forth his fruit in season; his leaf also shall not wither; and whatsoever he doeth shall prosper.
Therefore the ungodly shall not stand in the

judgment, nor sinners in the congregation of the righteous.

For the Lord knoweth the way of the righteous; but the way of the ungodly shall perish.
Psalm 1 KJV

In the year that King Uzziah died I saw also the Lord sitting upon a throne, high and lifted up, and his train filled the temple.

Above it stood the seraphims: each one had six wings; with twain he covered his face, and with twain he covered his feet, and with twain he did fly.

And one cried unto another, and said, Holy, holy, holy, is the Lord of hosts: the whole earth is full of his glory.

And the post of the door moved at the voice of him that cried, and the house was filled with smoke.

Then said I, Woe is me! For I am undone, because I am a man of unclean lips, and I dwell in the midst of a people of unclean lips: for mine eyes have seen the King, the Lord of hosts.

Then flew one of the seraphims unto me, having a live coal in his hand, which he had taken with the tongs from off the altar: and he laid it upon my mouth, and said, Lo, this hath touch thy lips, and thine iniquity is taken away, and thy sin purged.

Also I heard the voice of the Lord saying, Whom shall I send, and who will go for me? Then said I, Here am I send me. **Isaiah 6:1-8 KJV**

Go to the ant, thou sluggard; consider her ways,

and be wise: which having no guide, overseer, or ruler, provideeth her meat in the summer, and gathereth her food in the harvest. **Proverbs 6:6-8 KJV**

Train up a child in the way he should go: and when he is old he will not depart from it. **Proverbs 22:6 KJV**

Wherefore I say unto you, All manner of sin and blasphemy shall be forgiven unto man: but the blasphemy against the Holy Ghost shall not be forgiven unto man.

And whosoever speaketh a word against the Son of man, it shall be forgiven him: but whosoever speaketh against the Holy Ghost , it shall not be forgiven him, neither in this world, neither in the world to come, **Matthew 12:31 & 32 KJV**

The Lord is not slack concerning his promise as some men count slackness; but is longsuffering to us-ward, not willing that any should perish, but that all should come to repentance. **2 Peter 3:9 KJV**

For God so loved the world that he gave his only begotten Son, that whosoever believeth in Him should not perish, but have everlasting life.

For God sent not his Son into the world to condemn the world; but that the world through Him might be saved.

He that believeth on Him is not condemned but he that believeth not is condemned already, because he hath not believeth in the name of the only begotten Son of God. **John 3:16-18 KJV**

The thief cometh not, but for to steal, and to kill, and to destroy: I am come that they might have life, and that they might have it more abundantly. **John 10:10 KJV**

Jesus saith unto him, I am the way, the truth, and the life: no man cometh unto the Father, but by Me.

If ye had known Me, ye should have known My Father also: and from henceforth ye know Him, and have seen Him.

Philip saith unto Him, Lord shew us the Father, and it sufficeth us.

Jesus saith unto him, Have I been so long time with you, and yet hast thou not known Me, Philip? He that hath seen Me hath seen the Fathers; and how sayest thou then, Show us the Father. **John 14:6-9 KJV**

There was a certain rich man, which was clothed in purple and fine linen, and fared sumptuously every day: and there was a certain beggar named Lazarus, which was laid at his gate, full of sores, and desiring to be fed with the crumbs which fell from the rich man's table: moreover the dogs came and licked his sores.

And it came to pass, that the beggar died, and was carried by the angels into Abraham's bosom: the rich man also died, and was buried; and in hell he lift up his eyes, being in torment, and seeth Abraham, afar off, and Lazarus in his bosom.

And he cried and said, Father Abraham, have mercy on me, and send Lazarus that he may dip the tip of his finger in water, and cool my tongue; for I am tormented in this flame.

But Abraham said, Son, remember that thou in thy lifetime receivedst thy good things, and likewise Lazarus evil thing: but now he is comforted, and thou art tormented.

And besides all this, between us and you there is a great gulf fixed: so that they which would pass from hence to you cannot; neither can they pass to us that would come from thence.

Then he said, I pray thee therefore, father, that thou wouldest send him to my father's house: for I have five brethren; that he may testify unto them, lest they also come into this place of <u>torment</u>.

Abraham said unto him, they have Moses and the prophets; let them hear them.

And he said, Nay, father Abraham: but if one went unto them from the dead, they will repent.

And he said unto him, If they hear not Moses and the prophets, neither will they be persuaded, though one rose from the dead. **Luke 16:19-31 KJV**

For I am persuaded, that neither, death, nor life, nor angels, nor principalities, nor powers, nor things present, nor things to come, nor height, nor depth, nor any other creature, shall be able to separate us from the Love of God, which is in Christ Jesus our Lord. **Romans 8:38 & 39 KJV**

Know ye not that the unrighteous shall not inherit the kingdom of God? Be not deceived: neither fornicators, not idolaters, not adulterers, not effeminate (men dressed like women), nor abusers of themselves with mankind (homosexual) , nor thieves, not covetous, nor drunkards, nor revilers, not extortioners (swindlers) , shall inherit he kingdom of God. **1 Corinthians 6: 9-11 KJV**

For the flesh lusteth against the Spirit, and the Spirit against the flesh: and these are contrary the one to the other: so that ye cannot do the things that ye would.

But if you be led of the Spirit, ye are not under the law.

Now the works of the flesh are manifest, which are these: Adultery, fornication, uncleanness, lasciviousness, idolatry, witchcraft, hatred, variance, emulation, wrath, strife, sedition, heresies, envying, murder, drunkenness, reveling, and such like: of which I tell you before, as I have also told you in time past, that they which do such things shall not inherit the kingdom of God.

But the fruit of the Spirit is love, joy, peace, longsuffering, gentleness, goodness, faith, meekness, temperance: Against such there is no law. **Galatians 5:17- 23 KJV**

If we say that we have no sin, we deceive ourselves, and the truth is not in us.

If we confess our sins, he is faithful and just to forgive us our sins, and to cleanse us from all unrighteousness.

If we say that we have not sinned, we make him a liar, and his word is not in us. **1st John 1:8-10 KJV**

I am Alpha and Omega, the beginning and the end, the first and the last
Blessed are they that do his commandments that they may have right to the tree of life, and may enter in through the gates into the city.
The Revelation 22:13 - 14 KJV

If these are only but a few of the quotes from the Bible and what many of our past presidents said or thought about how our Republic is supposed to operate then we must ask, **"What changed?"** Did our current leaders begin to think they were smarter than our founding father or they were smarter than God? There is an old saying that says, "If you do not believe in God you'd better be right because agony and torment for eternity is a high price for being wrong."

We are a spiritual being and our soul will last for eternity either in heaven or in hell. Therefore it behooves all of us to know everything that is in the Holy Christian Bible because this is how we are to behave and the standards upon which our nation was founded. When we deny this fact or do not nurture our souls then we will suffer the consequences.

Please read and reread the scripture verses presented above and do your own research and I believe you will be convinced that our founding father made the right choice when they used the Holy Christian Bible as their model in establishing our wonderful Republic.

Probably the most telling quote above is the one by Theodore Roosevelt. I guess he saw it coming that if the nation was not careful we would forget what made us great and unique in the first place.

There is a theory that everything is in a state of decay. Everything works like a bell shaped curve. Everything starts fresh and green or alive and kicking. Then things begin to be better and riper. Then the best is picked or used up and then things begin to decay and then die. The only way you can stop or prolong this decaying process is to prune the plant or in our case retrain or bring in new blood and get rid of the old dying ways. Our founding father knew this and put in place checks and balances to keep bringing in new blood and keeping our government agencies from getting to the point that they just as well be dead as to what they do for the people they are supposed to be serving.

Also our founding fathers knew that our Constitution would only work or rule moral people_and our people were to learn "How they should live" from the Holy Bible. They even went so far as to state that America was formed based on Christian principles.

Therefore we have crossed over to the other

side of the bell shaped curve and are speeding toward destruction. Our only salvation is to start again beginning to teach the Holy Christian Bible. Not as a state religion but as how all American are to behave as our national standards. Those that object ask them to come up with a better set of moral laws that man should live by.

A couple of examples, that the Bible talks a lot about, that are causing us undue trouble and are lowering our moral standards out of sight. The first of these is fornication. Fornication is sex outside of marriage. It seems to be common, even in my own family that nowadays a couple meets, kisses and then moves in together as man and wife. There is no courting to really find out if you are going to be able to live with each other as long as you may live. If the couple finds out that they really don't like each other and want out they just split up and leave. No thought seems to be given to any children that came from this trial marriage. Somewhere around 40% of the white babies are born out of wedlock and somewhere around 70% of the black babies are born out of wedlock. Our young people remind me of a bunch of boys (like dogs) are roaming around looking for some female in heat to have sex with. This having sex and leaving the female to raise these unfortunate children is coming back to haunt us.

Two pictures recently came across my PC. One showed a lady in Kenya with a bunch of baboons climbing all over her car trying to destroy it. The second picture showed a bunch of out of control teenagers climbing all over a cop car trying to destroy it. This is the kind of image that come across my mind when I see all the rioting, looting, killing and burning of businesses down. I then ask myself whose children are these. Where are the parents that raise children to think it is okay to destroy other people's property? Are we raising a bunch of baboons? It surely seems so.

The following came across my desk as I was writing this book trying to get all Americas to understand that Standards of living are necessary for our nation to keep from going completely out of control. I believe it reflects what is going on in too many sectors of our society.

"Police Retraining.

Now let me see if I have this right.

There's no guidance or discipline in the home. 'Junior' doesn't even know where to send a Father's Day card. Junior gets dumped into the education system where he is socially promoted because the overwhelmed school district can't deal with the undisciplined whelp. Junior's major formation influences are 'gangsta' rap videos and a corresponding peer group of gangsta wannabes.

At age 18, junior is turned loose on society carrying a bad attitude, a broken compass and no respect for authority. Junior get himself in big trouble with the law because he is illiterate, unskilled, unemployed and his only source of income other than government assistance is illegal and meets dire consequences. Then, the situation diagnosis is that the police need more training compassion, sensitivity and understanding?

Pardon me for asking, but do you really believe this?"

Our government is, in a great part, causing all this fornication because they are paying to bring up these unfortunate children who have three strikes against them at birth. Where are the fathers that are supposed to be taking care of the children they bring into this world? Therefore by condoning and paying for the results of fornication our government is dooming a large portion of our people to eternity in hell for disobeying God's Holy Word.

We can stop or drastically or at least slow down this "free sex" society we created by having the government stop paying to raise children who were sired by males that are nowhere to be found. address and his Social Security number on the birth certificate. This way men that sire children can be held responsible for that child. Fornication cannot totally be stopped but we as a nation do not have to pay for the results of this activity that will doom many of our citizens to hell. With the money we spend on condoning "Free Sex" we could probably set up and fund free retraining centers across the country for those whose skills have been obsolete or those who need a skill to obtain a marketable skill that they can make a living using these skills.

The second sin that will doom our people to hell according to the Bible is_homosexuality. The Holy Bible clearly states that homosexuals will not inherit the kingdom of God. Yet look at all the laws and rights we are giving to those who clearly sin in the eyes of God. Did all the Presidents I have quoted above ignore the fact that homosexuality was a sin? Do you think they just blocked the sections in Romans and First Corinthians out and said they did not believe God was serious when he talks about homosexuals?

Let me be frank. Can you think of a more discussing activity than a man sticking his penis into the rectum of another man and calling it love? The penis and rectum are for eliminating waste or impurities from our body. If you want to spread a disease then homosexuality is a great way to spread a disease and spread it fast. If the Bible spends a great deal of time not condoning homosexuality, why then are we trying to make it seem okay to condone disease spreading activities? Have we gone mad and why are we trying to slap God in His face when He has total control over mankind? I am not sure what women homosexual do but one can only imagine.

Here are a few verses that our political and judges seem to have forgotten or over looked. I guess they think God does not mean what He says.

Thou shall not lie with mankind, as with womankind: it is abomination. **Leviticus 18: 22 KJV**

If a man also lie with mankind, as he heth with a women, both of them have committed an abomination: they shall surely be put to death: their blood shall be upon them. **Leviticus 20:13 KJV**

And there were also sodomites in the land: and they did according to all abomination of the nations which the Lord cast out before the children of Israel. **1 Kings 14:24 KJV**

For this cause God gave them up unto vile affections: for even their women did change the natural use into that which is against nature: and likewise also the men leaving the natural use of the women, burned in their lust one toward another; men with men working that which is unseemly, and receiving in themselves that recompense of their error which was meet.
And even as they did not like to retain God in their knowledge, God gave them over to a reprobate mind, to do those things which are not convenient. **Romans 1:26-28 KJV**

On the bright side:
I beseech you therefore brethren, by the mercies of God, that ye present your bodies a living sacrifice, holy,

acceptable unto God, which is your reasonable service.
Romans 12: 1- 2 KJV

If men and women desire to go against natural law as given by God and want to doom themselves to hell then let them do it in private and not try to get the rest of us to condone their nasty and discussing activities. Do your own research and see what the Bible has to say about homosexuals.

Of course there are other sins clearly spelled out the Bible but we put people in jail for murder, stealing, lying etc. So why do we condone fornication and homosexuals? As we have become fat our nation has had time to engage in impure activities and then begin to try to make it okay to do these nasty activities. If we required all our people to work hard and earn their own living, instead of the government taking care of them, then we would eliminate some of our impure activities.

We must also never forget that all sin is forgiven for those who seriously repent. The only sin that is not forgiven is rejection of the Holy Spirit (Holy Ghost in KJV.). The scriptures tell us that it is not God's desire for any to perish by all to come to repentance. Fornicators and homosexuals can be forgiven and receive eternal life if they repent, accept Jesus Christ as their Lord and Savior, and turn from their wicked ways. But yet we pay fornicators and we condone homosexuals. Much true thought needs to be

111

given to these two subjects because they are taking up too much time and energy when this time and money could go toward better projects.

Therefore ponder why our founding father used the Holy Christian Bible as their guide to establishing our unique Republic. Then take a look at the way we are currently operating our government and the way many of our homes have only one parent in them.

One Standard for all!

Ye shall have one manner (standard) of law, as well for the stranger, as for one of your own country: for I am the Lord your God. **Leviticus 24:22 KJV**

And when they (Jesus and His disciples) had sung a hymn, they went into the Mount of Olives.
Mark 14:26 KJV

Tell Me the Old, Old Story

1. Tell me the old, old story of unseen things above, of Jesus and his glory, of Jesus and His love. Tell me the story simply, as to a little child; for I am weak and weary, and helpless and defiled. Tell me the old, old story. Tell me the old, old story. Tell me the old, old story of Jesus and His Love.

2. Tell me the story slowly, that I may take it in - That wonderful redemption, God remedy for sin. Tell me the story often, for I forget so soon; the early dew of morning has passed away at noon. Tell me the old, old story. Tell me the old, old story. Tell me the old, old story, Of Jesus and His love.

3. Tell me the same old story When you have caused to fear, That this world's empty glory is costing me too dear, yes, and when that world's glory Is dawning on my soul, Tell me the old , old story: "Christ Jesus makes thee whole. Tell me the old, old story. Tell me the old, old story. Tell me the old, old story of Jesus and His love.

LEADERSHIP

The rich ruleth over the poor, and the borrower is
servant to the lender.
Proverbs 22:7 KJV

The Bible clearly gives us plenty of instructions dealing with leadership that every father and mother should take heed and teach them to their children. Listen very closely to these Scripture verses. I am sure there are plenty of others but these will give us a good start on how we should pick our leaders and how we can judge how well they are leading our blessed country. Special note should be given by our **American News Media** as they are reporting on the character of our leaders and how well they are doing.

General instructions:

Hear O Israel: The Lord our God is one Lord: And thou shall love the Lord thy God with all thine heart, and with all thy soul, and with all thy might.

And these words, which I command thee this day, shall be in thine heart: and thou shalt teach them diligently unto thy children, and shall talk of them when thou sittest in thine house, and when thou walkest by the way and when thou liest down, and when thou risest up.

And thou shalt bind them for a sign upon thine hand, and they shall be as frontlets between thine eyes.

And thou shall write them upon the post of thy house, and on thy gates. **Deuteronomy 6: 4-9 KJV**

Commentary:

In my book the good Lord is pretty specific about what he wants us to do with his Holy Words.

Family Matters:

Therefore shall a man leave his father and his mother, and shall cleave unto his wife: and they shall be one flesh. **Genesis 2:24 KJV**

Wives, submit yourselves unto you own husbands, as unto the Lord.

For the husband is the head of the wife, even as Christ is the head of the church: and he is the savior of the body.

Therefore as the church is subject unto Christ, so let the wives be to their own husband in everything.

Husband, love your wives, even as Christ also loved the church, and gave himself for it; that he might sanctify and cleanse it with the washing of water by the word.

That he might present it to himself a glorious church, not having spot, or wrinkle, or any such thing;

116

but that it should be holy and without blemish.

So ought men to love their wives as their own bodies. He that loveth his wife loveth himself.

For no man ever yet hated his own flesh; but nourisheth and cherisheth it, even as the Lord the church: for we are members of his body, of his flesh, and of his bones.

For this cause shall a man leave his father and mother, and shall be joined unto his wife, and they tow shall be one flesh.

This is a great mystery: but I speak concerning Christ and the church.

Never let every one of you in particular so love his wife even as himself, and the wife see that she reverence her husband.

Children, obey your parents in the Lord: for this is right.

Honor they father and mother; (which is the first commandment with a promise;) that it may be well with thee, and thou mayest live long on the earth.

And, ye fathers, provoke not your children to wrath: but bring them up in the nurture and admonition of the Lord. **Ephesians 5:22-33 & 6:1-4 KJV**

Commentary:

Can you think of a happier family where the husband loves the wife as Christ loved the church and where the children obeyed a loving father that was not cruel to them? The word cleave means adhere, or remain loyal or stick fast. What family member would not love to live in a family where the father loved his family as his own body? Read and reread this as the model for our American families.

Governmental leadership:

Here are the instructions given to Moses on the kind of leaders he needed to help him. I have also included God's instructions to Joshua after he took over after Moses death. And finally God's instruction to the new leaders of the first Christian Churches. Our people and especially our American News Media need to use these instruction to evaluate the qualification of those that want to be our local, state and national leaders. Particular attention needs to be given to the election of our Presidents.

• The kind of leaders Moses was told to seek.
Moreover thou shalt provide out of all the people able men, such as fear God, men of truth, hating covetousness: and place such over them to be rulers of thousands, and rulers of hundreds, rulers of fifties, and rulers of tens. **Exodus 18:21 KJV**

• God's instructions to Joshua after he took over from Moses.
Only be thou strong and very courageous, that thou mayest observe to do according to all the law, which

118

Moses my servant commanded thee; turn not from it to the right hand or to the left, that thou mayest prosper whithersoever thou goest.

This book of the law shall not depart out of thy mouth; but thou shall meditate therein day and night, that thou mayest observe to do according to all that is written therein: for then thou shalt make thy way prosperous, and then thou shall have good success.

Have not I commanded thee? Be strong and for a good courage be not afraid, neither be thou dismayed: for the Lord thy God is with thee whithersoever thou goest. **Joshua 1:7-9 KJV**

• God's instructions to the new leaders of His new church.

This is a true saying, if a man desires the office of a bishop, he desireth a good work.

A bishop then must be blameless, the husband of one wife, vigilant, sober, of good behavior, given to hospitality, apt to teach; not given to wine, no striker, not greedy of filthy lucre; but patient nota brawler, not covetous; one that ruleth well his own house, having his children in subjection with all gravity; (for if a man know not how-to rule his own house, how shall he take care of the church of God?") not a novice, lest being lifted up with pride he fall into the condemnation of the devil.

Moreover he must have a good report of them which are without; lest he fall into reproach and the snare of the devil. **1 Timothy 3:1-7 KJV**

While putting down my understanding of how God would have us live I have looked for what is said about our leaders in Washington, DC. So far I have not heard one person or read one article about the character and qualifications of our leaders. I particularly have not heard of anyone serving in Congress being called a righteous man or women. In addition I have not heard anyone talk about what kind of people God wanted as our leaders. Have we just rejected God's wisdom and who we should select as our leaders and how they should conduct themselves? Note that early on in this book it was stated that our founding fathers thought we should elect Christians as our leaders.

It seems that if we are going to ever become a moral behaving country, pleasing to God, there should be some universal understand of who we should elect as our leaders. As far as I can determine there is no such current understanding of the qualification we should seek in our leaders other than what the Bible has to say about the subject of leadership. If there are any traits which our leaders supposed to have in order to be elected in America, I could not find them. Maybe this is true because God wanted us to use His standards.

If you really want to know how well a person is going to do as a national leader look at the way he handles his family. How well behaved are his children and how much does his wife love him and how much does she back him up in what he undertakes. A man's family life is probably the best judge of how good a leader will be if elected. The same would go for any women that wants to run for public office.

One possible way of America achieving the standards God expects us to live by, is understanding the Biblical meaning of **Love** and then teaching it to our children and all our people. In America we refer to love making as love, and mother's love as love. We even refer to the feelings we have toward a family member or close friend as love. When the Bible uses the word love it is usually referring to unconditional love or the way God loves us. Our closest understanding of this here on Earth is motherly love. Our mothers love us regardless of what we do and we will always be their children who they dearly love and only want the best for them.

God loved us so much, yet while were sinner, that He gave His only begotten Son to die for our sins so that all who believed in His son would have eternal life. This is unconditional love as God sees it. It is not God's desire for any to perish but all to come to repentance.

The following is a set of scripture verses that are frequently used in wedding ceremonies. It deals with the real meaning of love as God see it. In the King James Version of the Bible, which I am using, love is translated as "Charity" which when you think about it, it is not a bad use of the meaning of love. When you read the word charity in these Bible verses think of love, the unconditional love of God. These verses should be taught in every grade in our schools from the lowest to the highest.

*Though I speak with the tongues of men and of angles and have not **charity**, I am becoming as sounding brass, or as tinkling cymbal.*

*And though I have the gift of prophecy, and understand all mysteries, and all knowledge; and though I have all faith, so that I could remove mountains, and have not **charity**, I am nothing.*

*And though I bestow all my goods to feed the poor, and though I give my body to be burned, and have not **charity**, it profiteth me nothing.*

***Charity** suffereth long, and is kind; **charity** envieth not; **charity** vaunteth not itself, is not puffed up, doth not behave itself unseemly, seeketh not her own, is not easity provoked, thinketh not evil; rejoiceth not in iniquity, but rejoiceth in the truth; beareth al things, believeth all things, hopes all things, endureth all thing..*

***Charity** never faileth; but whether there be prophecies, they shall fail; whether there be tongues, they shall cease, whether there be knowledge, it shall vanish away.*

For we know in part, and we prophesy in part.

But when that which is perfect is come, then that which is in part shall be done away.

When I was a child, I spake as a child; but when I

became a man, I put away childish things.

For now we see thought a glass, darkly; but then face to face; now I know in part; but them shall I know even as also I am known.

*And now abideth faith, hope, **charity**, these; but the greatest of these is charity.* **Chapter 13 of 1ˢᵗ Corinthians**

Can you think of a better attitude toward life than the above? What a glorious nation we would have if these verses and ones like them were taught to all our children and people on a continual basis. If I have to place any blame I would put it squarely on our recent past presidents and our recent and current members of Congress for being so blind as to think we can survive as a country worth living in without the Word and love of God constantly preached and practiced in all sector or our society. Forget the atheist. Instead of trying not to hurt their feelings we should feel sorry for them because they will spend eternity in torment and agony for denying God. Instead we must make sure all our people know what God expects of us. Again as I will state from time to time all sin can be forgiven if we repent and turn from that sin. Giving lip service to a sin and not changing just will not get it.

Much of the blame for all the wickedness in our society can squarely be placed on members of Congress for continuing to promote fornication by paying to support poor unfortunate children born out of wedlock with no godly father to direct their path. We must ask ourselves where the young adults and teenagers came from that riot, loot and burn down other people's property. What kind of love is there in these individuals? To make my point the next time you visit a class room in your local school ask how many of the children present live with two parents that are actually their biological parents. Because of our government we are going to have to live with these kind of unfortunate children as our future leaders that are growing up mad at the world with very little love in their heart. Looting, rioting and destroying other people's property surely is not showing one's love toward themselves, their family and especially the community and country they live in.

Where do we go from here?

If any person in a position of authority is reading this and denying our people access to the Word of God by failing to teach their children and their students they had better give some serious thought as to how they will spend eternity. If they are teachers at any level or handing down a court decision that discourage the use of the holy Scripture they may be looking at spending eternity in hell. Read the Scriptures and see if I am not right. Of course our teachers, political leaders and judges can repent. Then search the scriptures to learn how God would have us deal with His Holy Words.

Do you think God was only kidding when He says if we deny Jesus Christ, God will deny us? Children, America's leaders are playing with hell and the destruction of America as we know it. Go ahead and warm up to the atheist and those who deny God and go to hell with them. Of course even atheist can repent and turn form their wicked ways. Just don't die before you repent and have a chance to change.

We have a bright future because God is always willing to forgive our sins. But we must repent and turn from our wicked ways. If we continue to make nasty and sinful practices okay, legalize immoral behavior then we'd better begin to check out the hills and mountains because they may be the only safe place to go to when God just lets loose Satan on us to have his way with us.

"Oh, that will never happen says many!"

Read the Holy Scriptures and see what God has done with wicked people in the past. We can keep spending more than we take in to fund people who will not work, allowing our elected officials to milk our treasury for all it is worth, over taxing those who produce the jobs for our people, over regulate our people and paying women to have babies out of wedlock and we will continue on the downward spiral toward a totally immoral and bankrupt nation.

If we are truthful with ourselves it is our News Media that is totally responsible for the wickedness now going on in our country. I wonder how many of our Editors know the least little bit about how God would have us live and what kind of people God would have running our country. They two will be replaced and God will find another way of informing His people on "How then shall they live" and what standards God expects us to live by. If I were a member of our American News Media I'd be the first to check out the mountains as to where to hide when God finally has had it with us and just does away with us.

Here a few things our news media needs to be screaming about.

• Our Federal debt that is running the price of everything beyond many citizens ability to pay is totally out of hand. Housing is beyond most young people's ability to buy and have a nice place to raise a family. The price of groceries goes up every week. It cost more to run our cities and counties thus the taxes continue to rise making it near impossible for older couples to pay the taxes on the houses they have owned for many years. Do I need to go any further?

• The Federal taxes on our businesses and industry are so that many businesses are taking their business overseas and thus stealing jobs from our American citizens.

• Many businesses have to hire extra people to keep up with Federal regulations and thus taking money from the business that could be spent on production of goods and services.

   • Every year our government grows and we never lay off any governmental people whether we need them or not.

   • American News Media, I hope you are getting the message. You have fallen down on the job of being our countries "Watch dog."

As Abraham told the rich man in Lazarus and the rich man, **"You have the Scriptures, read them."**

The fastest way to turn our nation around is with strong righteous leadership in our top government jobs.

And when they (Jesus and his disciples) had sung a hymn, they went into the Mount of Olives.
Mark 14:26 KJV

1. My hope is built on nothing less Than Jesus blood and righteousness; I dare not trust the sweetest frame, But wholly lean on Jesus' name.
2. When darkness veils His lovely face, I rest on His unchanging grace: In every high and stormy gale, my anchor holds the veil.
3. His oath, His covenant, His blood Support me in the whelming flood: When all around my soul gives way, He then in all my hope and stay.
4. When He shall come with trumpet sound, O may I then in Him be found! Dressed in His righteousness alone. Faultless to stand before the throne!

Refrain:
   On Christ, the solid rock, I stand: All other ground is sinking sand; all other ground is sinking sand, Amen.

POWER

The Lord is high above all nations; and His glory is above the heavens.
Psalm 113: 4 KJV

This chapter is the most important chapter in this book. It is what advantage "Born Again" Christians have over the rest of the world. Unless the scales are taken off your eyes this is pure foolishness. Let us hope and pray that this chapter will remove the scales off your eyes and you will see clearly, "How them shall I live.".

It seems that man is constantly seeking power over each other and many times when a person gets a little power it goes to their head and it becomes the ruin of them. There is a power that all of us can use that does not hinder us and is the most valuable asset we can have. It is called the Holy Spirit. Just before Jesus left the Earth to go back to heaven He told His disciples that He would send them a Comforter (Helper) that would remind them of all that He had taught them and even more so they could do even greater things than Him. Since God has revealed Himself to us as God the Father, God the Son and God the Holy Spirit, the Comforter is God on Earth in the form of God's Holy Spirit or God with us. What greater power could you have than having

God with you all the time?

During my teenage years my father took me aside and told me that there was a power available that if I did not use it I would miss the better part of my life. He was talking about the Holy Spirit. I therefore have taken advantage of this power all my life since then.

How do you get it? When you accept Jesus Christ as your Lord and Savior and repent of your sins then He sends the Holy Spirit into your life to guide you in the ways you should go. This is called being *"**Born Again**"*. The kicker is repent and repent means to change and in this case change so that you follow God's commandments and precepts as best you can. When you fall short you should repent and ask forgiveness. As I have already said several time before in this book all sins that are repented of can be forgiven except the rejection of God's offer of salvation.

How does it work? When you tune into the Holy Spirit He reminds you of the things you should be doing and remind you not to do the things that are sinful and will bring harm to you. I feel that the greatest asset the Holy Spirit provides is that when you ask him to guide you toward a certain goal or something you want to do He will begin throwing ideas into your head and keep doing this until you have accomplished what you wanted to do. Many of my ideas from the Holy Spirit come while I am sleeping. I wake up the next morning knowing how to solve whatever problem that is facing me.

You have to be careful what you ask for because the Holy Spirit may give it to you. He also may ask you to do something you should do that maybe you will not want to do but it is the right thing to do. When I am building something and tune into the Holy Spirit He will give me ideas of how I can do it better or keep me from messing up. This maybe sound foolish but when I lose my hammer while building something I ask the Holy Spirit to show me where my hammer is and He will show it to me.

As I have be writing this book the Holy Spirit has shown me Bible verses to use that I had not thought about before and He has also suggested subjects I should bring up. One thing that you have to watch out for is that satan is also present in this world and he will also but ideas into your head. Therefore be care what you think you are hearing. The Holy Spirit would never ask you to do anything against the will of God.

From a practical point of view what do you think would happen if member of Congress sought the Holy Spirit before voting on each bill or when creating a new bill? How about the President when advising the many Federal agencies? What would happen if they also sought or tuned into the Holy Spirit when they thought about a new regulation, etc.? You see the Holy Spirit has many advantages. What greater advice could you get than advice from God? Remember the Holy Spirit is **God with us**.

The greatest advantage and use you can get out of tuning into the Holy Spirit is when you constantly study the Holy Christian Bible and know what is written therein you really learn and understand "How then shall I live?" I have been studying the Bible all my life and my prayers are answered in Scripture. I seem to know before I speak or do something evil that I am not supposed to be thinking that way or doing what I am about to do thanks to the Holy Spirit.

Therefore if you want to have the greatest power that is in this world then accept Jesus Christ as your Lord and Savior and repent. Then listen as the Holy Spirit begins to speak to you and begin to lead in the paths of righteousness. I can promise you that when you become a Child of God you will begin to thirst for the things of God and you will not get enough of what God has to say to you. With the Holy Spirit dwelling in you, you will begin to lead a contented and productive life.

Here are a few verses of what the Bible has to say about the Holy Ghost (Spirit).

Sending the Comforter:

Verily, verily, I (Jesus) say unto you, He that believeth on Me, the works that I do shall he do also; and greater works that these shall he do; because I go unto My Father.

And whatsoever ye shall ask in My name, that will

I do, that the Father may be glorified in the Son.

If you love Me, keep My commandments.

And I will pray the Father, and he shall shall give you another Comforter, that He may abide with you forever: even the Spirit of thruth; whom the world cannot receive, because it seeth Him not, neither knowest Him: But ye know Him, for He dwelleth with you, and shall be in you.

I will not leave you comfortless: I will come to you.
John 14: 12-18 KJV

Howbeit when He, the Spirit of truth, is come, he will guide you into all truth: For He shall not speak of Himself; but whatsoever He shall hear, that shall he speak: and He will shew you things to come. **John 16:13 KJV**

Coming of the Holy Spirit:

Just before Jesus Christ left Earth He gave His disciples instructions about when the Holy Spirit would come. These are His instruction and the results as related in scripture. The power and importance of the coming of the Holy Spirit was demonstrated by coming with great power in the form of tongues of fire resting on each person to indicate that this is a personal matter and each person has to accept God offer of salvation individually.

Until the day in which He was taken up, after that he through the Holy Ghost had given commandments

133

unto the apostles whom he had chosen: to whom also he shewed himself alive after his passion by many infallible proof, being seen of them forty days, and speaking of the things pertaining to the kingdom of God: and being assembled together with them, commanded them that they should not depart from Jerusalem, but wait for the promise of the Father, which, saith he, ye have heard me. **Acts 1:2-4 KJV**

And when the day of Pentecost was fully come, they were all with one accord in one place.

And suddenly there came a sound from heaven as of a rushing mighty wind, and it filled the entire house where they were sitting.

And there appeared unto them cloven tongues like as of fire, and it sat upon each of them.

And they were all filled with the Holy Ghost, and began to speak with other tongues, as the Spirit gave them utterances. **Acts 2:1-4 KJV**

Born Again:
When a person accepts God's offer of salvation it is called being born again. This means that you become a new person and the old sinful self without hope of eternal life dies and you become a new person with the hope of eternal life with Christ in heaven.

There was man of the Pharisees, named Nicodemus, a ruler of the Jews: The same came to Jesus by night, and said unto Him, Rabbi, we know that thou art a teacher come from God: for no man can do the miracles that thou doest, except God be with him.

Jesus answered and said unto him, Verily, verily, I say unto thee, Except a man be born again, he cannot see the kingdom of God.

Nicodemus saith unto Him, How can a man be born when he is old? Can he enter the second time into his mother's womb, and be born?

Jesus answered, Verily, verily, I say unto thee, Except a man be born of water and of the Spirit, he cannot enter into the kingdom of God.

That which is born of the flesh is flesh; and that which is born of the Spirit is spirit.

Marvel not that I said unto thee, Ye must be born again. **John 3:1-7 KJV**

Gifts of the Spirit:

When you accept Jesus Christ, by faith, (or have been born again) as your Lord and Savior with repentance then you are given gifts to further the kingdom of God or help build the church. I also believe these gifts can be used in our everyday life in living out the time ordained for us to live. Listen as I present these scripture verses and see where your gifts are. Maybe you have other gift as modern times come to pass. But whatever gifts you have use them as best you can and even improve on them and you will live a contented and productive life pleasing to God.

Here are the scripture verses I found dealing

with God given gifts.

For I(St. Paul) say, through the grace given unto me, to every man that is among you, not to think of himself more highly than he ought to think; but to think soberly, according as God hath dealt to every man the measure of faith.

For as we have many members in one body, and all members have not the same office: so we, being many, are one member one of another.

Having then gifts differing according to the grace that is given to us, whether prophecy, let us prophesy according to the proportion of faith; or ministry, let us wait on one ministering: or he that teacheth on teaching; or hethat exhoreth, on exhortation: he that giveth let him do it with simplicity: hethat ruleth with diligence; he that sheweth mercy, with cheerfulness.

Let love be without dissimulation. Abhor that which is evil; cleave to that which is good. **Roman 12:3-9 KJV**

Wherefore I give you to understand, that no man speaking by the Spirit of God calleth Jesus accursed: and that no man can say that Jesus is the Lord, but by the Holy ghost.

Now there are diversities of gifts, but the same Spirit.

And there are differences of administration, but the same Lord.

And there are diversities of operation, but is the same God which worketh all in all.

But the manifestation of the Spirit is given to every

man to profit withal.

For to one is given by the Spirit the word of wisdom; to anther the word of knowledge by the same Spirit; to another faith by the same Spirit; to another the gift of healing by the same Spirit; to another the working of miracles; to another prophecy; to another discerning of spirits; to another divers kinds of tongues; to another the interpretation of tongues; but all these worketh that one and the selfsame Spirit, dividing to every man severally as he will.

For as the body is one, and hath many members, and all the members of that one body, being many, are one body; so also is Christ. **1 Corinthians 12:1-12 KJV**

Every good gift and every perfect gift is from above, and cometh down that the Father of light, with whom is no variableness neither shadow of turning. **James 1:17 KJV**

Fruit of the Spirit:

When you use your gifts to the glory of God then you will receive these fruits as evidence that God is working in our life. What a glorious world this would be if everyone in America showed evidence of using their God given gifts to the glory of God and man.

Here are the verses I found dealing with the fruit of the spirit.

But the fruit of the Spirit is love, joy, peace, longsuffering, gentleness, faith, meekness, temperance" *against such there is not law.* **Galatians 5:22 & 23 KJV**

Commentary:

The Bible is full of other material dealing with the Holy Spirit and it could be a life time study to try to learn all that the Bible has to say about the works of the Holy Spirit. It would be a worthwhile study for any one that wanted to take on such a study. I can personally testify that when you tune into the Holy Spirit and allow Him to lead your life you will live a content and productive life. You will sleep better and you will even feel better because of the stress of being found out about your sins and ill feeling will be gone. Of course you will still sin and fall short of the glory of God. But the way of repentance has been revealed to you and you can clear the air immediately and go on living the life given to you. Try it and experience the power that goes along with having the Holy Spirit riding with you everywhere you go.

You can put your new life in action by joining Bible teaching church. If you cannot find one try to find a Bible Study group of like believers and meet once a week and go verse by verse through the Bible. Some groups find it more interesting in studying what the Bible has to say about a particular subject.

If you cannot find a church or Bible Study

group then start one on your own in your own home. But try to find at least one long time "Born Again" Christian to help lead your new group. In any case you will be blessed by learning more and more about how God would have you live. I can assure you that there will be much joy in heaven when each of us come to the knowledge of the saving grace of Jesus Christ.

Just think what a change there would be in Washington, DC if all our elected officials attending a serious week Bible Study so they could compare their actions to what they found that God would have them run our blessed country.

After reading this chapter I hope you begin to realize why our founding father created our Republic using the Bible as their guide. There is historical records that show the whole Congress went to Devine services, as they called it, in the early days of our Republic.

God's power should be desired by everyone!

PROBLEMS AND SOLUTIONS

The wicked flee when no man pursueth: but
the righteous are bold as a lion.
Proverbs 28:1 KJV

While beginning to think about the problems
facing America I stopped and though about how
blessed we are as a nation with everything a
human being could possibly want, for the taking,
if one is willing to do what is necessary to enjoy all
these benefits. Then I cut on the TV or read the
morning paper and see all the evil that is going on
in our nation and realize that man has not
learned one thing since the beginning of time. I
have come to realize that man is self- destructive
trying to be one up on his neighbor. Man's only
hope in living a contented and productive life is
with the proper restrains and clear standards to
live by. Therefore all our problems originate by
man not living by the commandments and
precepts given by God. In the early days of Israel
they had no king or ruler. They only had judges to
settle their petty disputes. When they got a king is
when all hell broke loose. Because of their hard
heads God finally sent foreign kings in to scatter
them all over the world. If we all did what God
expected of us we would need very little
government. All we would need is agencies to

provide the services we cannot provide for ourselves. But because only a few do what is right when no one is looking we need a government. But any government will fail when the leadership does not make sure all our people know the rule God expects us to live by. Therefore since we have eliminated God's commandment and precepts from all public sectors or government controlled units we are reaping the whirlwinds. Let us all hope this book will bring attention to why we are experiencing so much trouble in our beautiful country.

To complain without giving a solution is like blowing the wind or about as worthless as a bucket of spit. Therefore I am giving what I think are the major problems facing America with my suggested solution. Ponder what I have presented and see if I am not telling the truth.

What a glorious nation America we would be if all of us would often ponder on the meaning of "Righteousness" and then tried to live as if we understood the meaning. The problems we have in America all are rooted in the lack of righteous living by many of our people and **especially our leaders.** Therefore the solution to all our problems is found in the Holy Christian Bible upon which America was founded. If we are to continue to receive God's under deserved grace we must all constantly drop to our knees and seek God's guidance on **"How then shall we live?"** Of course nothing will happen if we all knew all wisdom and did nothing to correct what is wrong with our country. We must never forget that it is people that cause most of our problems with the exception of a few storms here and there. Therefore we must seek out and elect and appoint the best **"Righteous Doers"** in our midst as our leaders and support them in making the right decision for our people. We must make sure we do not tempt any leader we pick by keeping him or her in power too long so they will not fall into the trap of **"Power corrupts and absolute power corrupts absolutely"** and **fall into disgrace** like many of the disgraceful people we now have in power that have been there too long that their judgment is clouded.

"Righteousness"is a term I hope I hear a lot of in the future!

Now let us take our problems one by one as I see them.

Lack of understanding and knowledge of how God would have us live as demonstrated by the way many of our people are living:

If we are to sustain our American way of life all our citizens need to know what kind of nation we live in and how and why it was founded. The only way this can happen is for our public schools to teach our children the standards we are expected to live under from the first grade and continue thought out all of our educational institutions. These courses should be required courses where only a high score would be acceptable. Without such subject matter being stressed and all our people understanding what is expected of them we can truly expect chaos and reaping of the whirlwind.

Of course, like I have presented several ways so far in this book, the standards we are to live by are found in the Holy Christian Bible. In our present 2015 situation we are getting more and more away from things of God. **Have we gone mad?** Just look at the misery and the number of our own citizens we have in jail and in our prisons and ask yourself way. Did those in jail and prison not know what was expected of them? You would think not! Whose fault is this? The fault should be placed squarely on our parents and our school system. Of course nothing will happen and the misery index will continue to climb totally out of control until we realize our problems.

The solution to our bad behavior is the lack of knowledge of how God would have us live and the consequence of not living by God's commandments and precepts. We can buy into the concept of "Separation of Church and State" and we will continue to decline morally until we self-destruct. If we honestly look back at the beginning of our blessed nation we will find that our founding fathers wanted the Bible to be taught in our schools. They just did not want the government forcing people to believe in any kind of religion and to worship or believe in any kind of religion. But they did want our citizens to know what was in the Bible because that is where the standards they expected us to live by were found.. They did not want a state run church and they did not want a Pope telling us what to do or not to do. But again, they wanted our people to know what was taught in the Holy Christian Bible as the standards we all to live by.

One last fact along these lines. I graduated from high school in 1955. There was a religious air about our school in the way the school administrator wanted us to behave. If you misbehaved you either got a paddling or had to write something 1,000 times. After each of these events you would decide not to do what you did to get punished. Plus, if you got in trouble at school you got in trouble at home. Before graduation we had a religious service where all graduates were expected to attend. A local preacher came and gave a talk along the lines of what I have been trying to get across in this book. The point of this paragraph is that there were rules we were expected to live by. It might sound strange in that I remember the first time I heard someone curse publicly and the first time I heard of anyone getting pregnant out of wedlock. I also do not remember anyone in my class that did not live with both their natural parents and everyone I knew went to church as a family. This might sound like a pipe dream. But we must ask ourselves, "What happened to the stability of family life in the past 60 years?" What standards do we now live by?

Results:
Here are the results of not having any standards to live by as I see them.

• Family life
Our nation is made up of families. Therefore our nation's future is a strong as our families are. To give us some idea of how strong our families are we should take a count in our First grades, Eighth grade and our Twelfth grades and see how many of our students are living with both biological parents. These figures should be published in every American newspaper and broadcast on every TV and radio station very often to bring to the attention of our citizens the breakdown of our families.

Keep in mind that our future leaders will come from these broken homes where few eat as family together. If they do the TV is on and the meal is interrupted by one or more members looking at their cell phones or whatever you want to call all these electronic devices everyone seem to have now a days. The dinner table is where, in the past, wisdom was passed on from the parents to the children. Also it has not been long ago when a blessing was asked before the meal began thanking God for providing the meal before them. Also family problems and concerns were discussed and talked about. This is where the family standards of behavior were handed down. Just think what the country misses when parental wisdom and standards are not passed down to the children. As a grandparent I try to pass down the wisdom I have gained over my 78 years to my grandchildren as often as I can. When is the last time you got a young person aside and told them what the good Lord expected of them? In many cases it is obvious that some children have not been taught any restraint by their uncontrolled and disruptive actions.

Therefore all our national problems can be found to begin or show their ugly head when there is a breakdown in the family. I can think of no greater joy than when my children and grandchildren are found living as close as they can according to the Will of God for our people. I was pleased beyond words when my children graduated from college and took the place in the workforce of our nation. I was likewise saddened when two of my grandchildren met someone, kissed and then moved in with each other without getting married. I am holding my breath that no children come from these unions and my grandchildren just decide to go their separate ways.

I recently learned that my 50 year old son that lives in another town was elected Deacon in a large local church. I could not be happier. This showed me that the community in which he lives have put their trust in his leadership along with the other Deacons serving in that church.

Our nation will only be as strong as our families!

• **Polite Language:**

As time passes by the language of our people has become less polite showing a total disrespect for the will of God. Words and phrases like "sh*t" "pissed off" the "F" word and Lord help us when they take the Lord's name in vain. I cry for these people because they do not know what they are doing and the consequences, thereof. These are but a few that are becoming far too common. You also hear these words on TV and on the radio as if they are common language. Some TV shows that are supposed to be funny use curse words in every sentence and people laugh and laugh. I am no goodie, goodie but I have lived long enough to know that people that use bad language lack character and I often worry about what they spend their time thinking about. **"As a man thinketh so does he doeth"** is a known fact and this should concern every one of us.

The Lord doesn't like ugly!

• **Fornication:**

Men and women have been having sex with each other since the beginning of time whether they were married or not. But God clearly tells us that if we have sex outside of marriage we **will go** to hell unless we repent. Repent means to turn from. So you cannot repent and keep on having sex outside of marriage because that is not how it works. On the island I live on there are only several thousand full time residences. A couple of days ago the local churches got together and passed out school supplies and school uniforms to children whose parents could not afford them. The count was around 80 children that were helped. Only mothers brought their children and not a male was in sight. From time to time I have helped with this project and have always been impressed with the blank faces on these unfortunate children. I don't know what goes on in the families of these children but it is obvious that these children, by their actions, have not been inspired and nurtured as all children should be. The lack of fathers in so many of our families is going to be our downfall. We must ask why this is such an accepted practice? Have we forgotten that these children will be running our nation when some are mad at the world for being treated so badly?

Sex is designed for marriage!

• Church Attendance:

Much is said about separation of church and state but the local churches have been the one thing that has held our families together for generation. But somehow we are experiencing a reduction in church attendance. In the past when someone got sick, wanted to get married or have their children baptized they called on the local preacher. But now we must ask how many people are getting married in our churches and how many children are being baptized. If a large sector of our people are not receiving any religious training by not going to church where will they learn the standards we are to live by? It is God's commandment to keep the Sabbath Day Holy.

• Drugs:

There would be no "Drug Lords: if our citizens were not using them. Recently one of our high state officials was caught having drug parties in his home and was removed from public office and spent some time in prison. You would have to ask what kind of parents do the ones using drugs have. Maybe we should legalize all drugs and treat them like alcohol and anyone with a blood showing too much drugs in their system should be put in jail or pay a very large fine.

Has anyone realized that we can get high doing service work? Most of us get much pleasure help others instead of receiving ourselves. Another way we can get much satisfaction and pleasure is learning all God has to say about a certain subject. There are plenty ways of getting high instead of frying our brains with drugs.

Drugs should be used to cure us instead of killing us!

• **Too many people on the government dole.**

When someone does not have to work for what they receive they have too much time on their hands and thus get in trouble by losing self-respect. They then begin to ask what else free is the government is going to do for them. They also begin to vote for those that will keep the money and perks flowing toward them. Before long you have a mess that soon gets out of control. Our people then become slaves to the government by the government having too much control over their lives.

Welfare should be for the very sick and those that really can't work!

• **Lack of an education worth anything:**

When children come from broken homes with little or no supervision and no stable family life they are hard to deal with when they come to school. Many have no respect for authority and often disrupt the class rooms. The public schools have to deal with these poor unfortunate children and in many cases just promote them regardless of the grades they make just to get rid of these children. The tragedy of all this is that these are the children that will be running our government. How much do you think adults raised under these conditions will care about the people they are supposed to be taking care of? They are more likely to milk the system for all its worth as they saw being done during their youth.

No one should graduate from our public school without a <u>marketable skill</u> to add to our workforce!

• **Not required to defend our nation.**

When we removed the draft we missed the opportunity to give our young people some of the best training available for our young people. In the service they learned discipline and what it means to be responsible for one's actions and behavior. Drill instructors were the best things that ever happen to a human being. In the service our young people go into the service undisciplined and come our as a gentleman ready to take their place in society. They respected authority and are conditioned to do their part and carry their own weight. They also learned that they had to depend on other people for their own safety and thus learned to get along in all situations. Therefore we did a great disservice when we stop requiring all 18 years olds to serve some time in our armed forces.

Every young person should spend sometime in the service before they go into the workforce.

• Few pay any taxes or no taxes:
Many of our people pay no taxes. They use our roads, send their children to public schools and are protected by our armed forces. Therefore how can they appreciate what our country does for them if they don't pay to support it?

All Americans should pay a percentage of their income in taxes for being an American.

• Social Security ~ Too many people on disability.
There is no longer a Social Security Fund. The money people now pay into the so called Security Fund goes into the Federal treasury and then paid out of the general fund. Each person no longer has a Social Security account and is paid according to some kind of schedule that has little to do with how much money you put into the fund. You can also apply for disability and get funds out of the Social Security fund when maybe you paid very little into the fund. Therefore our

government has robbed the Social Security fund and is not investing that money for the ones that paid into it.

Our government robbed the Social Security fund!

• **Abortions:**

One of the disgraces in modern time is the killing of our unborn. What kind of animals have we become that we think it is okay to kill our unborn? There is a verse in the Bible that reads like this when it is talking about the end of the world as we know it. Listen and cry because it seems truer than ever.

And because iniquity shall abound, the love of many shall wax cold. **Matthew 24:12 KJV**

We must ask ourselves why would a woman want to kill the life that is growing in her womb? This is no small problem because in recent years we have killed millions of unborn children and are even so cold that some are selling baby part of those killed during abortions. Has fornication become so wide spread that our people say, "Let's have sex and if a baby comes of the free sex then we will just have an abortion." What kind of women would be willing to kill in cold blood, from within her own body? Also what kind of man would make a woman pregnant and then leave the women and child to fend for themselves. Yes, large portions of our people seem to have grown cold without any love in their heart.

Here is some insight of what Jesus thought about children.

And they brought young children to Him, that he should touch them: and His disciples rebuked those that brought them.

But when Jesus saw it, he was much displeased, and said unto them, Suffer the little children to come unto Me, and forbid them not: for of such is the kingdom of God.

Verily I say unto you, whosoever shall not receive the kingdom of God as a little child, he shall not enter therein.

And He took them up in His arms. Put His hands upon them, and blessed them **Mark 10:13-15 KJV**

What a glorious day it would be in America if we thought as much of little children as Jesus does.

Our children are our future; every one of them is needed!

• **Divorce/Adultery:**

Why do we have so many divorces in America? Most men like women and most women like men. Many just don't like the one they are married too. Is it that many marry before they really get to know the one they are about to marry. Maybe our people should not be allowed to get married unless they have known each other for at least one year. The Bible has much to say about how married couples should act toward each other. I have already added these instructions in another chapter. Go back and look at them. The Bible says a man should love his wife as much as he loves his own body. Pretty strong language. Since most couples have children then the children get pushed around after a divorce. What a shame!

Instead of accepting the fact of many divorces resulting in many children that feel deserted and not loved much thought should be given to why we have so many divorces. It was certainly not God intention for married people to get divorces. In fact how God sees marriage is covered three places in the Bible. Ponder on these.

Listen as God speaks to us.

Therefore shall a man leave his father and his mother, and shall cleave unto his wife, and they shall be one flesh. **Genesis 2:24 KJV** (Cleave means adhere – adhere means remain loyal or stick fast)

The Pharisees also came unto Him (Jesus), tempting Him, and saying unto Him. Is it lawful for a man to put away his wife for every cause?

And He answered and said unto them. Have ye not read, that He which made them at the beginning made them male and female, and said. For this cause shall a man leave father and mother, and shall cleave to his wife: and they twain shall be one flesh?

Wherefore they are no more twain, but one flesh. What therefore God hath joined together, let not man put asunder (into separate pieces or separated).

They say unto him, why did Moses then command to give a writing of divorcement, and to put her away?

He saith unto them, Moses because of the hardness of your hearts suffered you to put away your wives, but from the beginning it was not so.

And I say unto you, whosoever shall put way his wife, except it be for fornication, and shall marry another, committeth adultery; and whose marrieth her which is put away doth commit adultery. **Matthew 19:3-9 KJV**

So aught men to love their wives as their own bodies. He that loveth his wife loveth himself.

For no man ever yet hated his own flesh: but nourisheth and cherisheth it, even as the Lord the church: for we are members of his body, of the flesh, and his bones.

For this cause shall a man leave his father and mother, and shall be joined unto his wife, and they two shall be one flesh. **Ephesians 5:28-31 KJV**

The good Lord comes down hard on adultery. He meant for people to stay married and puts most of the obligation of keeping the marriage together on the man saying a man should love his wife as much as Christ loves the church and gave his life for it. Listen closely to these verses dealing with adultery. Do you think God was just kidding when he had these words written?

Thou shalt not commit adultery. **Exodus 20:14 KJV**

And the man that committeth adultery with another man's wife, even he that committeth adultery with his neighbour's wife shall surely be put to death. **Leviticus 20:10 KJV**

Know ye not that the unrighteous shall not inherit the kingdom of God? Be not deceived neither fornicators, nor idolaters, nor adulterers, nor effeminate, nor abusers of themselves with mankind (Homosexuals), nor thieves, nor covetous, nor drunkards, nor revilers, nor extortioners, shall inherit the Kingdom of God. **1 Corinthians 6: 9 & 10 KJV**

Divorce and adultery are not in God's plan for man!

Solution:

I am writing this the day after the Fox News Republican debate held in Cleveland, Ohio on

August 6, 2015. What impressed me the most was the lack of what the cause of most if not all our nation's problems. Of course all our problems stem from sin, the kind of problems facing our nation listed above. We can help solve these problems by good leadership in high places in our government to set the tone of how he or she expects our citizens to live out their lives. A good example by our President, members of Congress and our governors will go a long way toward developing a more moral society.

Of course electing righteous men and women to serve as our President, members of Congress and our governor would help. Therefore much attention and research should go into who we elect as our leaders.

The next factor in helping to create a more moral society is our News Media. If they did their job we would not be electing men and women that want to be in office for the monetary benefits it brings.

Finally, the most important is our families.

The more families we have where the mother and father make sure their children understand what God expects of them and the consequence thereof the better the chance of us creating a more moral society. Again, saying over and over again, when we elected men and women from strong righteous families we will have a better chance of our society becoming a more moral society.

Therefore the key to all our problems in America is electing confirmed moral people to lead us by example and by frequent encouraging words. Again none of this will work without strong families rising up righteous men and women to serve as our leaders.

This maybe a pipe dream but of course nothing will happen and we will continue to go down the tube unless it is a national priority and things are put in place that will accomplish the goal of a more moral acting citizenship.

Ponder these thoughts about our all important American families.

• Even if a family reads the Bible and has family Bible studies what the parents teach their children at home are trumped by the government removing all mention of anything to do with God in all our public sectors. Peer pressure from a child's friends often takes our children of in the wrong direction. But the pressure from our government, especially our teachers and professors go a long ways toward brain washing our children to thinking there is nothing to God and they can do just about anything they want to do and no one will care or take notice.

• By the government paying for children born out of wedlock they created families that there is no father to guide these sad children. It seems by now someone in our government would catch one. Or do you think members of Congress

160

continue this practice thinking those on welfare would vote to keep them in power? What a sick thinking society we have become to keep us such distorted practices.

• All the while our American News Media sits by and does not do their research and report what is happening to our families. I guess they have been brained washed and also do not believe in God and His will for our people.

Each American family is a link in the chain of success of our nation!

• Our second problem is our Washington, DC government and our State governments that think liberalism is the way to go.

The time has come for our American citizens to vote out anyone that has been in office over two terms. The day of professional politicians is over_and we need to go back to a government run by the people where we send the best and brightest to Washington, DC to oversee our many government agencies to make sure they are serving our people economically and efficiently. Serving our people is the concept that all government employees should have when doing their job. The term **"Public Servant"** should precede the name of all government agencies.

The way our Federal government has evolved we now have a government that has gone far from the intent of our founding father to the point that we are playing with destruction. Instead of having outstanding citizens from each community or region representing us for one or two terms we have representatives that have been in office far too long. You would think many of our current representative's think that our citizens owe them a living and as many perks as they can think without any regard for the needs of the people that voted them in office. The terms that are often referred to this group are **"The Establishment"** and members of the "Reelection Cult."I guess you would say we have gone back to having "Lords" and "Earls" lording over us peasants. As a result our Federal government has grown out of control and now cost more than we can afford. We no longer have a government **"For the People_"**and it is now certainly not run **"By the People"**.

Results:
   • As of the middle of 2015 we have a 18 trillion dollar Federal debt. Have you ever thought about how big a trillion dollars is? It has not been long ago that a million dollars was a lot of money. Now billions of dollars to fund one bill is not unheard of. I don't think I have ever heard about members of Congress or the President talking about where the money is going to come from when they present a new bill or how they are going to enforce or implement a new regulation. We just go ahead and borrow the money to fund

whatever programs that some splinter groups wants so they will vote to keep some Congressman or Senator in power. Or at least fund some Congressman or Senator's next reelection.

• Our Federal agencies keep getting bigger and bigger and seem to lord over us more and more with this regulation or that regulation. Our tax code is a disgrace. When is the last time we had a mass layoff in our government. It seems once you are hired by the government you have a life job no matter what you do or don't do. Try getting something done through the government and be prepared to wait weeks, months or even years while some Federal employee makes sure they take their coffee break. I guess our Congressman and Senator don't want to rock the Federal agencies because all these people vote. If a Congressman or Senator votes to not fund an agency then those people working in that agency will not vote for them. The cycle goes on and on and the government gets bigger and bigger and it requires more and more money to run it. Money we don't have so we just go out and borrow it or print more money thus reducing the value of our dollars and prices for everything goes up. Round and round goes our governments, with not one perk left out.

• Our federal government gives out grants and foreign aid from money they have to borrow. Now you tell me the sense in that!?

• It seems that no bill is voted on by any Congressman or Senator unless it has something to do to keep them in office.

• Because of the creation of the "Establishment" and the "Reelection Cult" our government is broken.

Solution:

• We need to search far and wide for a strong conservative leader in the White House that is not a politician that has vast business connections and is known for getting things done efficiently and economically. We need a leader that will not be afraid to purge our government for unneeded agencies and people that are bringing our country down.

• We need to elect from among our people strong leaders as our members of Congress, preferably non politicians.

• We need to put in term limits so that no member of Congress can serve more than two terms. It would be okay if they served more than two terms if they had a two year layoff between serving in Congress. This way they would be forced to get out among our people and see the results of poor governing.

• We need a balance budget Amendment so that we cannot run up shameful debts like we now have.

• While searching for strong leaders to elect to high position we need to keep the concept of "Righteousness" in mind when considering the one you should vote for. How a man or women handles their own family would be a good place to start. If one cannot handle their own family how can the handle the vast responsibility that goes with a public position?

• It would be nice of the ones we vote for knew what God has to say about "How we should live". Since our country was founded upon the Bible then our leaders should know why our founding fathers used the Bible as their guide in established our blessed Republic. Our founding fathers even use the Presbyterian form or government to pattern the way we run our government.

• I guess you can say that we need strong righteous leaders to run our government taking turns editing and overseeing our government and then return home to contribute to the community the take out of.

Our third problem is the lack of strong and dedicated American News Media to be our forth branch of our government, our "Watch Dogs".

Things in the government would not get out of hand if those running our government knew that we had many eyes looking over their shoulder and reporting the least little infraction in the way they are handling the people's business. There seems to be very little investigating and seeking the truth of things going on in our news media. They seem to flack to the killing of a black by a white police and forgetting all the other tragic deaths going on in America. Little is reported about what the Federal debt does to the retired people on fixed income. If the Democrats or liberal do anything out of order it is not reported. But let a conservative or Republican do something out of order and we have a national uproar. It is not the truth of something it is the charge. Our news media seems to convict many people before the truth is known. They ruin a policeman who shoots a person before they knew that the person had committed other crimes over and over and was trying to bring harm to the police. You never read in our papers or watch it on TV how man picks members of Congress who have voted for themselves without the voters input. You never hear how the moral decay of our country keeps increasing because we have tried to remove the teaching of God's commandment and precepts everywhere possible. You never hear about where the grant money came from to build this local building or that building. I guess you would say that our present American News Media is about as worthless as the hind tit of a "Bo Hog" and far as trying to keep our government doing what they were sent to Washington, DC to do.

Results:
  • We have a government out of control.
  • The moral decay of our country continues to grow. "Pissed off" is now used in polite

conversation and nobody turns their head. Couples now kiss and jump in the bed and no one is worried about the children of this unstable union.

• No one is watching the barn door. Therefore anything now goes and our people have learned how to break the Federal Treasury. They seem to not understand that when they do this they doom themselves along with everyone else.

Solution:

We need someone to come up with a way to inform our citizens of what is going on in our government as to what is right and honorable and to do it in such a manner to run our current American News Media out of business for not doing their job as our "Watch Dogs." I predict that this is not far off in our future. America has a need for such a movement and in a free society all demands will be met. I hope that if some young person is reading this he or she will pick up the scent or demand and run with it. It is sad to see our American News Media go down the drain. But if you don't cut it then it is time to go.

Summary:

We have three problems that only strong national leaders can solve. Again, we have families that are falling apart, our national leaders are letting us down and our news media is not doing their job. Let us hope and pray that a strong leader will come forward and set the example that will get us back on track of how God would have us live.

National Righteous Leadership is Our Only Hope!

SUMMARY

When the righteous are in authority, the people rejoice: but when the wicked hearth rule, the people mourn.
Proverbs 29:2 KJV

As far as I am concerned and from where I sit and observe what is going on in America I believe our current President (2015) and members of the "Reelection Cult" in Congress are absolutely worthless. The proof is clear by the size of our government, the over burden of regulations, our national debt and all those Americans receiving Government assistance. If something is not done about these factors shortly we will run out of money and our great "Free Enterprise System Experiment" will go down the drain and our nation of the people, by the people and for the people will become something man only dreamed about for a few hundred years. The old adage of **"Power corrupts and absolute power corrupts absolutely"** Is showing it ugly head and consume us all. We will just eat our seed corn and lie down and die as a once great nation where **"One Nation Under God"** became a lie.

In my life time (born 1937) I have seen the dollar become more and more worthless, the Social Security fund raided, and the size and burdensomeness of government out of control. Children are having children and the government is paying to support these unfortunate children. Drugs are everywhere and our streets are no longer safe. Looting has become common and everyone seems to be disabled and cannot work and the government believes them. Gas prices have gone from below 25 cents a gallon, to over $3.00 a gallon. We must ask why? There was a church on every corner and now when you say you go to church every Sunday and sometimes during the week many ask why and wonder why there are so many divorces and people living together before they are married. Many teenagers and young adults are out of control and killing each other. Now all we talk about is how someone feels and his rights but never ask about his duty and obligation to do right in the sight of God and mankind and make them accountable to the Government which supports them.

What we seem to not understand is that we can and will be replaced if we don't begin to clean up our act and get back on the path of righteousness.

What else can I say? Except we have lost our way and our future looks bleak from where I sit and observe what is going on, If I look off in the future I can see a glorious future full of contented and productive people working together to create and keep a moral and hardworking society going. But sneaking up in the woods is our downfall if we don't wake up and once again learn what our founding fathers knew.

Glory and Honor or Destruction – Which will it be?

Being an old man and seeing how fast we are falling out of grace with God my bones have begun to hurt and my soul is crying out for the sake of my children and my grandchildren. I live in the country and when I go to town for supplies I want to stop all those cars going to and fro and ask them where they are going in such a hurry and why do they have to get where they are going this minute. I want to ask the guy that speeds past me on a curve, "Is getting there few minutes early worth risking your life?" A couple of weeks ago I was coming back from town with my wife and traffic was stopped dead and we had to wait about forty five minutes before traffic was allowed to continue. It seems the driver of a small fast car was speeding along doing something with one of these new hand held computer/telephones and crossed the center line and hit an oncoming truck carrying a camper head on. The driver died at the scene and several other people were seriously hurt and sent to the hospital.

Has our life gotten on such a fast pace that life does not mean anything to us anymore. I wonder how many young people know how to make a rabbit trap or even how to build a tree house out of malarkey lumber? I wonder how many of our children have ever sat on their front steps, looking up at the clouds and wondered how they got there and how so much beauty can be in such a wide open space in the sky. I wonder how many children know how many people died during the Second World War so that they are free to use their "Things" they all carry around talking to each other on these things instead of actually talking to each other and learning body language and how to get along. I wonder how many of our citizens wonder at all at how pleasant life can be if they only stopped and though a few minutes on "How then shall we live?"

We all have the opportunity to receive eternal life but many in America are living as though we did not have eternal souls that will live forever in heaven or hell. They ignore the fact that there is a God running things. All one has to do is look at the complexity of the natural world and they must agree that all this just did not happen. Even bird eggs hatch in seven, fourteen or 21 days in relation to how God set up Earth's cycles to operate.

Therefore all American, especially our elected official need to step back, take a deep breath, and ponder whether they are living and governing according to God's will for our nation. If we are all honest with each other we have a long way to go. God tells us that things that are not possible by man are possible by God. With a little honest study of the Bible and acting and governing accordingly we have a glorious future ahead of us. But if we continue on the same Godless path nothing but chaos and misery is our future.

Let us all hope that a great awakening will take place in America. Are you in or out? Like it or not you are in the game. Choose wisely.

EPILOGUE

One of the great generals of the Old Testament, Joshua, made this statement which would be a great and worthwhile attitude for all American citizens. Listen closely and take this into your very being.

Choose you this day whom ye will serve – but as for me and my house, we will serve the Lord. **Joshua 24:15 KJV**

The following are three verses that are at the heart of our current trouble. We are living as if there was no God and His commandment and precepts do not matter when His very Words will survive us all. It would be nice if we all were on the winning side of God. Our feeble attempt to go our way without God will fade away and we will be left with Satan trying to run everything and everyone. Maybe it is a time to wake up and revisit what God has to say in the Holy Bible as how we should live. If God had these words put three places in the Bible I am sure He especially wanted us to take notice.

Heaven and earth shall pass away: but My (Jesus Christ) words shall not pass away. **Matthew 24:35 KJV**

175

Heaven and earth shall pass away: but My (Jesus Christ) words shall not pass away. **Mark 13:31 KJV**

Heaven and earth shall pass away: but My (Jesus Christ) words shall not pass away. **Luke 21:33 KJV**

Maybe there is something to the fact that man shall not live by bread alone but by every word that proceeds out of the mouth of God (The Holy Bible). But there comes a time for action and that time is now. I like the way Solomon says it. I'll end with his words of wisdom.

To everything there is a season, and a time to every purpose under the heaven: A time to be born, and a time to die; a time to plant, and a time to pluck up that which is planted; a time to kill, and a time to heal; a time to break down, and a time to build on; a time to weep; and a time to laugh; a time to morn, and a time to dance; a time to cast away stones, and a time to gather stones together; a time to embrace, and a time to refrain from embracing; a time to get, and a time to lose; a time to keep, and a time to cast way; a time to rend, and a time to sew; a time to keep silent, and a time to speak; a time to love, and a time to hate; a time of war, and a time of peace. **Ecclesiastes: 3:1-8 KJV**

THE TIME HAS COME!

I strongly believe it is time we voted out all "Professional Politicians" and began to be governed by the brightest and most informed citizens from each community and region. We should send these representatives to Washington, DC and edit or oversee that all our government agencies to make sure they understand that they are "Public Servant" and are serving our citizens as efficiently and economically as possible. The time for "Professional Politicians" is now over. Any government agency or individual in these agencies that are not directly serving our citizens should be laid off immediately. The elected member of Congress should have the absolute authority to do away with a government agency that is not serving our citizens along with everyone working for these failed government agencies. The day of our government ruling over our people with no thought of their welfare should be over by their vote in the next election.

Use the Holy Bible as your Standards of Behavior and you will lead a contented and productive life.

PRAYER FOR THE PEOPLE

Good Lord our savior and creator of all mankind we lift your name above all Names and give you all the power, honor and glory you deserve as our one and only God. The Great I am!

Lord we whole heartily thank you for all that you have given us. Thanks you for our beautiful country you have provided for us to live in and bring up our families. Lord we thank you for the plenty and lack of want you have given our people. Lord we thank you for all the great and smart people we have in our blessed country. Lord we thank you for everything that we take for granted. Lord please remind us when we become ungrateful for all you have provided for us.

Lord we ask a special blessing on all our people and for all of them to think of you often and pray for your grace and guidance.

Lord we earnestly ask that you instill in all our people the need for you in their lives and cause a great awakening among all our people and especially our leaders. Please remind our leaders that it is You that put them in place to rule of our people as you would have them rule and protect our people.

We pray for all those that Satan has shut their minds off from you and doomed them to hell. We all know that it is not your desire for anyone to perish but for all to come to repentance.

Lord have mercy on all our people and impress

upon them all to become a praying and obedient people.

Finally Lord, we thank you for sending your only begotten Son to die for our sins that whosoever believed in Him would have everlasting life. Lord thank you for life itself and all the joys it brings to those who rely on you for their daily guidance. Lord have mercy on all our leaders and show them the benefits of abiding in your will for them individually and as a nation.

Thank you Lord for being our loving God that cares for all us even when we sin and fall short of your glory. In Jesus Christ name we make this prayer. Amen and Amen!

God bless you all, every one of you.

AUTHOR
SAM LYBRAND